Architectural Guide
Wrocław

Architectural Guide Wrocław

Marcin Szczelina

With additional contributions by Aaron Betsky, Ivan Blasi, Łukasz Kos, Kuba Snopek et al.

Contents

Photo: Philipp Meuser

Source: iStock (Santiago Rodriguez Fonto)

Foreword

Aaron Betsky

Wrocław is the city that could have been the model for a multi-cultural Europe. Once one of the largest and most multi-ethnic metropolises in Germany, it is now a second-tier, but beautifully preserved part of Poland. Spared most of the devastation that hit other cities in Europe during World War II, but transformed more than most of them by the political realities of the post-war period, Wrocław is a showcase of old, mainly German, architecture set in the hard casing of Soviet-style development and beset by a consumer-oriented banality that encroaches on its carefully preserved image of the past.

As Wrocław rose to prominence as a market town, it is fitting that the city's showcase is its market square. Huge in scale and busy with ornamentation, it makes room for the business of trade while showing off the translation of its profits in façades that present themselves in a riot of colours and profusion or details. There are few grander spaces in Eastern Europe than this.

That is not all that Wrocław was. Slicing through this wedding cake of bourgeois achievement, the Erich Mendelsohn-designed department store and other fragments of Modernism remind you that Wrocław was also once progressive and open to change. The vision of what the city could have become sits outside the core, brooding over a public park with a grandeur that belies the banal functions that take place within it today. The Centennial Hall is a monument to the future Wrocław never had and probably never will have. Wrocław is a city worth knowing, if for no other reason than to marvel at what was once an open, multi-cultural city whose character is still visible in its architecture. With Marcin Szczelina as a guide, the beauty of this place becomes clear and evident, even if its glories are so much in the past. But at night, it comes alive in other ways...

The author is the Dean of the Frank Lloyd Wright School of Architecture, Scottsdale and Spring Green.

Giraffes, fences and the Centennial Hall: narrative architecture in contemporary Wrocław

Source: Philipp Meuser

On Giraffes and Architecture

Ivan Blasi

A giraffe in front of the Centennial Hall in Wrocław is a rather surreal but also a common picture of the city. It reminds us of the photo of Villa Dall'Ava by OMA with the same animal. Contemporaneity is both complex and contradictory and Max Berg's structure stands to confirm that modern times were already anticipating today's uncertainty driven by technology and determining a state of permanent provisionality.

Poelzig, Scharoun, Berg, Tawryczewski and Grabowska-Hawrylak left an architectural legacy based on research, experimentation and improvement of living conditions that is well perpetuated by today's generation of architects. Having overcome the period of brick offshoring and formal reconstruction, the city propelled to rediscover its personality built from the flood of customs, arts and thoughts that continuously reach and cross it. This character configures contemporary Wrocław and accentuates its openness to culture, and courage as well as passion for change and innovation. The feeling of constant debate persists in the city's streets – bordered by a mixture of Gothic, Baroque, Modern, Soviet, post-Modern and contemporary architecture – and in the public, water and green spaces which for centuries have been the heart of its urbanism. Today's discussion on the Solpol by Jarząbek is a magnific symptom of this architectural debate among citizenship and an opportunity to undergo many of the city's actual urges. Other works have become part of the ordinary, waiting to be rediscovered in the next years like the city has recently done with the former air-raid shelter, today the Contemporary Arts Museum by ch+ architekci, the extension of the Renoma department store by Mackow Pracownia Projektowa and other works

OMA's famous giraffe picture

which have been nominated for the European Union Prize for Contemporary Architecture – Mies van der Rohe Award. Our social urban environment changes much faster than the physically built one, highlighting the importance of citizens in decision-making. The participation of Wrocław's inhabitants in its construction has given shared and collective visions, together with plans of action that will allow a continuous improvement. Giraffes in cities continue to look down on universities, parliaments, churches and urban development, but also on the rivers, parks and public spaces which are the places of meeting, discussing and proposing. If in the twentieth century architecture was photographed together with cars and other machines, today the giraffe may be a symptom of a certain return to the basics – architecture as the way to articulate spaces for living and for people's imagination to flow.

The author is coordinator of the European Union Prize for Contemporary Architecture – Mies van der Rohe Award.

Tumski Island Church

The Architectural Importance

Kuba Snopek

The uniqueness of Wrocław's urban plan

Most Polish cities are easily recognised by their medieval plan. At the centre one finds a big commercial square with public buildings. Adjacent to the square are dozens of orthogonal streets and narrow plots. The city is bound by an oval ring of defensive walls. But there is another feature that defines Polish cities: the degree of their destruction during World War II. Caught between Nazi Germany and the Soviet Union, and unprotected by geographic boundaries like mountains or sea, Polish cities suffered severe damage from 1939 through 1945. In many cases, Polish cities were so ravaged as to make destruction itself the most notable feature of their contemporary urban plans. Wrocław, the largest city in western Poland, is one of these.

After surviving most of the war unscathed, in just a few months of 1945 Wrocław was annihilated; in the years following the war, nearly all of the city's German inhabitants were forcibly removed and replaced by completely different people. These two intertwined events, the act of physical destruction of the city's buildings and the thorough relocation of its dwellers, defined what contemporary Wrocław has become in the second half of the twentieth century.

A city and a river

Since its beginning, the city was bound to the Oder River. The Wrocław bishopric was founded in the year 1000, and the sacral heart of the city, with its panorama of tall gothic temples, was located on islands in the Oder. In the thirteenth century,

Source: University Library in Wrocław

Map of the City of Breslau was completed in 1562 by Barthel Weihner

a regular city grid was imposed on the Oder's left bank, to the south-west of the Cathedral Island. This south-western quadrant, easy to access for merchants and travellers, became the principal vector of Wrocław's expansion. The city's main street, Świdnicka (German: Schweidnitzerstrasse), embroidered with Wrocław's most important public buildings of all epochs, also led south from the centre. For medieval Wrocław the Oder served as the citys northern limit.

In 1807 the Napoleonic officers ordered the destruction of the the city walls. This plainly military decision unleashed the city's expansion. For the next century Wrocław recorded an unprecedented growth – its medieval core was being gradually encircled with newer and newer layers of urban tissue. A belt of elegantly designed parks replaced the walls and surrounded Wrocław's historic central area. On the intersection of the green ring and the city's main streets, spacious squares were designed. In the late nineteenth century the built territory of the city increased tenfold, following

Source: University Library in Wrocław

Eastern part of *Breslau Market Square*, before 1900

the rapid industrialisation. Vast new neighbourhoods grew from all sides of the Old Town. Hundreds of new streets and housing blocks, embroidered with parks and public squares, formed large urban ensembles. A few decades later, in the early twentieth century, these bourgeois neighbourhoods were counterbalanced by ample worker settlements. Throughout the nineteenth century the Oder also changed the role it played in the city. From being Wrocław's northern frontier it evolved to an inner-city border, dividing the city into its richer south and poorer north.

Destruction

By the end of World War II, with Nazi defeat on the Eastern Front already inevitable, the city was declared a fortress: Festung Breslau. It was fortified and sent on a suicide mission to impede enemy forces and delay the Nazi defeat. For over three months, Festung Breslau saw extensive bombardment and intense urban combat. The city's geography, which had shaped its growth for a 1,000 years, now informed the way it was destroyed.

In 1945, destruction came from the south, following the main roads into the heart of the embattled city. During a three-month-long siege, Festung Breslau was annihilated, street after street, and house after house. The Oder framed the city's destruction, dividing it into two different spaces. The southwestern half, destroyed by fierce combat between Nazi and Soviet forces, lay in ruins. The medieval core of the city, along with its beautiful Napoleonic-era squares and nineteenth-century bourgeois neighbourhoods, were all gone. What remained were singular houses and shreds of pre-war urban planning – geometry of streets, remnants of the city's infrastructure, the urban green. The city's northeast – more difficult to access because of its location between two branches of the Oder – was left relatively untouched. Though some houses were bombed, dozens of urban blocks were preserved, among them entire urban ensembles of the late nineteenth and early twentieth century. An exception was the area converted into Festung Breslau's emergency airport during the war. Its runway carved from the urban tissue an oblong wasteland that eventually became today's Grunwaldzki Square.

This spatial division into the north and the south is crucial for understanding contemporary Wrocław. One who visits the city should be aware of which side of the river one finds oneself. North of the Oder there is predominantly pre-war

Aerial view of Breslau city centre, May 1945

Nowy Targ Square

Market Square

Solny Square

Source: University Library in Wrocław

Breslau Market Square, before 1945

Source: iStock (CCat82)

Wrocław Market Square, today

Breslau (the German name of the city) with some post-war intrusions. South to the river one is a guest of post-war Wrocław, with a few lonely reminders of the city's past. While the northern part has continued in strong relation to the historical city, the southern part has been built anew; after the war, the ruins of Breslau became a laboratory open for architectural experimentation.

Reconstruction

Post-war redevelopment in Wrocław was far more reckless than in Warsaw, Poznań and other destroyed Polish cities. Few monuments of heritage were reconstructed, many streets were lost or had their geometry changed, and in many places the historical partitioning of land was abandoned. The liberties taken in rebuilding Wrocław were caused in part by change of administration and a turn towards socialism, but most importantly they were caused by the complete change of population in the years after the war.
Immediately after the war hundreds of thousands of the city's German inhabitants were replaced by similar numbers of Poles. Thousands of families of the pre-war city were evacuated, killed during the siege, or banished after the war. The Poles who replaced them were also escapees. Many of them were forced to flee their homes from the areas incorporated into the Soviet Union. Thousands of families came back directly from Siberia and Kazakhstan, to where they had been displaced by the Soviets in 1939. Thousands fled from the areas of central Poland, destroyed by the war. Although it consisted mostly of Poles, this immigration was extremely diverse. The newcomers were both urban intelligentsia from big metropolises, as well as rural dwellers from remote regions. Together with these people came a multitude of distinct memories and rituals. They spoke different dialects and prepared different cuisines. The future rebuilders of Wrocław had different professional backgrounds and felt nostalgic about different regions of Poland.
One thing all of them lacked was an emotional relation towards the city to which they had moved. Architects, engineers and builders who were about to raise Wrocław from the rubble felt freer to act here than they would have in Warsaw, Poznań or Gdańsk. The reconstruction became a series of experiments that had one thing in common: an ambiguous relation to history. The architects didn't decide to simply rebuild the city as it had been, nor did they disregard the history and build everything from scratch. Instead, they used the urban past of the city as a material for further work and creative exploration – a method that can still be read in the work of Wrocław's architects today.
This approach showed in the first area in need of rebuilding: the medieval heart of the city. Its rigid orthogonal street structure, which had survived the siege, became the base for an architectural patchwork of contrasting approaches to post-war reconstruction. One of them was to give credit to history and rebuild what had been there before. But which history to rebuild? In Wrocław, this classic dilemma of heritage preservationists was warped by post-war trauma and the ascendant Communist political situation. The reconstruction efforts had to ignore the German past and also somehow graft themselves to the medieval Polish roots of the city. Two main medieval squares, Rynek and Solny Square, were subject

to this kind of reconstruction. At first glance, they seem like proper historical reconstructions: the historic plots and dimensions of the houses were preserved, along with the historic feel of their architecture. Yet a closer look reveals that many of the reconstructed buildings are works of pure imagination, historicist fantasies fuelled by nostalgia and the prevailing political agenda.

A contrasting strategy was used to rebuild the third important medieval square: Nowy Targ. An area of the Old Town surrounding this square had been entirely destroyed, and planners decided to abandon historical references. The architecture of the small housing estate raised in this area was to be modern in design. Simple, boxy houses covered a vast swath of Wrocław's Old Town. Their scale and delicate divisions on the façades are the only references to the history of the place. Together with the residential function of the housing estate, there came spatial components unseen in the medieval centres – greenery and spacious inner yards amongst fragmented urban blocks. Unique moments where those simple housing units join with the pre-war survivors (mostly on today's Szewska Street and Nankiera Square) are beautiful evidence of the ingenuity and sensitivity of the architects of that era. Nowy Targ Square itself is striking owing to its cosy scale and architectural consistency, both impossible to imagine today.

Another strategy was used to rebuild Kościuszki Square, first designed in the era of Napoleon. The rigid geometry of the square's plan and the streets running centrally through its façades bear resemblance to the squares of Paris, such as Place des Vosges or Place Vendôme. What was different, however, was the architecture surrounding the square. In the Parisian examples it was always an architectural ensemble with a consistent façade. In pre-war Wrocław the square was surrounded by a multitude of extremely diverse buildings. The reconstruction of the square gave a chance to fix this "mistake". The Socialist Realism that ruled in Poland in the early 1950s – a pompous, monumental and classicist style imposed on architects by Stalin – provided the perfect language in which to rebuild the façades of the square "as it should have been" – with classical splendour and absolute consistency. There is an important exception – on the most prominent plot of Kościuszki Square stands Renoma warehouse (aka the Wertheim Department Store, or PDT). This colossal survivor of the war breaks the rhythm of the square just enough to prevent spatial monotony – a typical feature of Stalinist ensembles.

Around the 1960s post-war reconstruction gained momentum on a much larger scale. The main building effort focused on the vast wasteland south and west from the Old Town. The southern nineteenth-century extension of Wrocław had been a vast and a carefully designed area. Its composition was formed by wide avenues – the principal axes of the neighbourhood. At their intersections, representative public squares were designed. Between this rigid geometry, the dense urban fabric was organised into orthogonal blocks with inner yards. The 1945 catastrophe wiped out almost all the houses, but the geometry of the streets was preserved. Two decades later, when the area was finally cleared of rubble, it was developed again – this time as a huge Modernist housing estate. The geometry of the plan was preserved, but used differently than before. Led by idealism and the Modernist Zeitgeist, the post-war architects decided to invert the urban fabric; what had formerly been an urban block with an inner yard now became a stand-alone building surrounded by greenery. Dozens of long prefab slabs were located diagonally within the footprint of the former urban blocks. Where it was not possible to fit them, there appeared tall residential towers of different widths and heights. One priority was to ensure enough light, space and greenery.

A key part of the southern extension was left empty. It is the so-called Southern Centre – a huge void aligned with Powstańców Śląskich Street, the main axis of the neighbourhood. In the last half century, the Southern Centre was reimagined many times, but it was never developed. Generations of architects imagined this territory as post-war Wrocław's most

A city and a river: Wrocław cityscape, 2015

representative area, a perfect place for big public spaces and high-rises. But there was never more than one skyscraper at a time casting shadow at the void of the Southern Centre. In times of communist Poland it was Modernist Poltegor, clad with golden reflective glass; a few years ago it was replaced by a taller – but still lonely – commercial tower.

A space that offers a full experience of Wrocław's post-war urban planning is a section of Krucza Street (between the streets Grochowa and Gwiaździsta). On one side it ends with a nineteenth-century church tower – a reminder of what had been there in the past – and, on the other, with Wrocław's only skyscraper. The street is surrounded by an abstract geometry of massive housing units across its whole length, and paved with cobblestone evoking the nineteenth century. Somewhere around its middle point, the street attaches to Hirszfelda Square – the pinnacle of 1960s inverted urbanism. What formerly had been a rectangular public square was filled with an elevated rectangular public building.

The 1980s and 1990s brought a major shift in dealing with the urban matter. The eras of Solidarity and *perestroika* marked an end to the Modernist tabula rasa approach to architecture. At this time, Wrocław's architects started showing a great amount of sensitivity towards their city's pre-war past. This meant shifting the focus to the northern, pre-war districts of the city. The movement to build so-called urban infills (Polish: *plomba* – a cavity filling) started. This dental metaphor explains aptly what these buildings were: infills in the pre-war urban fabric. Dozens of them appeared to close half-ruined urban blocks. In extreme examples – i.e. around Bema Square or Szczytnicka Street – the non-existent pre-war urban tissue was recreated completely with these kinds of intrusions. This fragmented campaign to refill the urban cavities was the first step to reassess the significance of the nineteenth-century remnants of German Breslau.

Today Wrocław is experiencing the imminent renaissance of nineteenth-century housing areas. Façades are gradually being renovated and inner yards reinvented. Some areas, i.e. those in proximity to Świętego Macieja Square, are experiencing moderate gentrification. Other places – like those next to the Technical University – a more organic upgrade.

Source: iStock (Mariusz Szczygiel)

One of the newest trends within contemporary residential architecture is a critical reinterpretation of late nineteenth-century urbanism. The newest examples of this approach can be found on the Kępa Mieszczańska island north-west of the centre. In the foreseeable future this trend of reinventing *Gründerzeit* urban blocks will continue.

The future

A few challenges await Wrocław in the close future. One of them is reimagining the areas designed for cars. Modernist architects saw the city's destruction as an opportunity to dedicate more space to roads. Today one can see that often they had carried their visions way too far. Left for future planners is the empty area to the east from the Old Town, known as Społeczny Square – a huge and senseless motorway-style junction built at the centre of the city. It joins with the Trasa W-Z (West-East Highway) – an ugly scar within the historic Old Town. Both spaces are in need of redevelopment. Both are challenging, but also offer incredible opportunities to create new urban spaces.

However, Wrocław's most difficult challenge will be to organise its memory and create a consistent strategy for the preservation of architectural monuments. For many decades following the war the non-Polish heritage of the city was disregarded. The shift of perception started by the architects in the 1980s was strongly reinforced by the Great Flood of 1997. Forced to fight with the forces of nature for their city, its inhabitants finally developed a strong emotional bond with Wrocław.
Today the pendulum of affection has swung all the way in the opposite direction. Wrocław's pre-war German architecture is being romanticised, while its post-war architecture and urban planning are commonly despised. The global trend of disregard for abstract and monotonous Modernist architecture in Poland is strengthened by the negative attitude towards the Communist past. The greatest challenge for Wrocław's present-day inhabitants is not only to preserve separate artefacts of post-war architecture and city planning, but also to imbue in the city's memory that which is most important about them – the affection for architectural experimentation.

Remnants of the foundations of a castle belonging to the Silesian Piasts

Photo: Philipp Meuser

The Foundations

Kamil Krawczyk

Source: School Sisters of Notre Dame

Gothic castle built between 1270 and 1290 under Henry the Righteous

The substantial relics of the foundations of a castle belonging to the Silesian Piasts, descendants of a Polish sovereign Bolesław the Wrymouth, were discovered within the cellars of the Monastery of the School Sisters of Notre Dame on St. Martin's Street in Wrocław. During the twelfth and thirteenth centuries it was the hugest stronghold in the Silesian district, the second after Krakow's Wawel as far as age and importance was concerned. The core of its dwelling part was a huge central building (with eighteen sides) from the time of Bolesław the Tall, Henry the Bearded and St. Hedwig. The cylindrical dwelling tower in Wrocław's stronghold is one of the two oldest brick buildings in Poland. It was built on the initiative of Bolesław the Tall who also initiated the transfer of brick technology from Western Europe to Silesia. This transfer indirectly took place through Saxony and Brandenburg, probably through one of the monastic building workshops. The building was extended into a longitudinal palace in the middle of the thirteenth century at the latest, during the period of Henry III the White. Earlier, near the palace, a central chapel with apses was erected. Next, a Gothic extension was built in the late 1280s during unification attempts and efforts to acquire the Polish crown undertaken by Duke Henry IV the Righteous.

The new Gothic palace differed from the previous one owing to the spectacular design of the central area and the presence of huge buttresses across its whole length. This extraordinary residence emerged as a result of the combination of the palace being built on a rectangular plan and the building being built on an octagonal plan. It had two axes of symmetry: longitudinal and horizontal. The latter was erected on the site on which the cylindrical building with eighteen sides had been demolished, in the meantime, to its foundations. The octagon was encircled with huge 5.5 m long buttresses. In the thickness of the northwest buttress there was an inner corridor, 1.65 m wide, that led to a *dansker* (toilet) situated on the side of the Oder River. The building probably housed a palace hall on the first floor.

The palace from the third part of the thirteenth century was joined by means of galleries with a chapel featuring four apses and a new chapel dedicated to St. Martin, also funded by Henry the Righteous. When it came to the layout of the palace hall as well as the topography of the most important buildings, it referred in its entirety to the palace of Charles the Great in Aachen. It can be treated as a manifesto of the duke's power at the time of his efforts to crown himself King. Undoubtedly, it was the most magnificent ducal residence in Poland during this period. At the same time it was an outstanding building in terms of originality in architectural form across Europe.

A fragment of the foundation

Photo: School Sisters of Notre Dame

Photo: School Sisters of Notre Dame

The basement – outer wall of the castle on the right

The last sovereigns of Wrocław, the Piast dukes Bolesław III and Henry VI, set about handing over both the adjacent areas and the castle to the Church as early as the first part of the fourteenth century. Over the passage of time the site of the former palace and chapel, situated to the north, was taken over by the canonical Courts of the Collegiate Church of St. Cross. The only remnant of the ancient stronghold is the northern escarpment of the fortification. From the middle of the nineteenth century onwards, the canonical Courts were incorporated into the huge neo-Gothic buildings of St. Ann's Monastery School (1856, 1860 to 1866 and 1891 by Joseph Ebers; redesigned in 1921 by Johannes Gebel and Theodor Pluschka). At that point its origins as a castle went largely unremarked.

Source: School Sisters of Notre Dame

Section of the tower built under Bolesław the Tall

Photo: School Sisters of Notre Dame

Central core of the dwelling tower

2

Modernist Achievements

Łukasz Kos

Wrocław's architecture and urbanism has been shaped as much by the shifting borders of the kingdoms and nations that it belonged to as by the influx of the people who and political systems which oversaw its development. Its history leading up to World War II was painted by occasional Polish influence and long spans of German and Bohemian bourgeoisie development. Its post-war fortunes behind the Iron Curtain fell prey to decades of negligent Soviet-style centralised planning. What resulted was an extreme swing of fortunes from the excesses of the pre-war bourgeois excesses to material depravity of the Cold War Socialist system. Despite the economically and politically harsh forty-four years following World War II, now Polish Wrocław saw a spur of Modernist architectural ingenuity. As a result, one cannot dismiss the influence of Polish architects from the post-war Socialist era to the 1,000 year urban history of Wrocław.

Four buildings worth noting are:

1 Marek Dziekoński's rotunda for the Racławicka Panorama, designed in 1965 and not completed until 1985, exemplified the ability of young Modernists to experiment with form and texture in an era of inept Soviet-style industrial planning that resulted in the twenty year construction period of this Brutalist experiment.

Photo: Philipp Meuser

4

Photo: Philipp Meuser

2 A pair of residential towers known as the *Sedesowce* (Toilet Seat Blocks) for their bold undulating elevations. Designed by Jadwiga Grabowska-Hawrylak in the late 1960s, they were an inventive response to the Communist Party's increasing demand for standardisation and repetition in the centrally controlled building industry.

3 Another pair of landmark buildings are *Kredka* and *Ołówek* (Crayon and Pencil), a student housing complex design by Marian Barski and Krystyna Barska which was completed in 1985. A testament to mass and scale, sloped roofs add an iconic sense of domesticity and playfulness to the imposing forms.

4 Finally, the *Trzonolinowiec* (a form of new speak that roughly translates as the Trunk and Cables Building) is more an exercise in engineering folly than it is in architecture. The eleven-storey residential building hangs from its concrete core by a series of cables. This type of

engineering is usually found in earthquake zones, yet somehow found its way into the centre of Wrocław during the 1960s. Wrocław's mosaic of architectural forms is a testament to its rich history. Take note of the beautiful follies from that painful era of communism as a testament to the human desire for lightness and pleasure at a period where there was very little of it.

3

Photo: Mariusz Szczygieł

Source: Igor Snopek / Architecture

Bird's-eye-view of the Mary, Queen of Peace Catholic Church

Architecture of the VII Day

Kuba Snopek, Izabela Cichońska, Karolina Popera, Nicholas W. Moore

Between 1945 and 1989, despite the Communist state's hostility towards religion, over 3,000 churches were built in Poland: the Architecture of the VII Day. Built by their parishioners, these churches represent a truly communal architecture, one which rejected the rigid, Soviet-style Modernism of the centralised state. Post-war Poland was a battleground of fiercely competing ideologies. Following the devastation of World War II, a paradoxical rebuilding of society took place, in which Poland's tradition-bound Catholicism met the fervent technocracy of Soviet Communism. Millions of conservative, religious people from small towns and villages became first-generation proletarians as they moved to industrial cities, newly built according to the functionalist Soviet template. Missing from the template was the parish church – the shared building which had anchored these newly industrialised communities.

Parish communities in Poland began to fill the spiritual void in the Communist plan. Neither legal nor prohibited, building churches engaged the most talented architects and craftsmen, who in turn enabled parish communities to build their own spaces of worship. The role of the architect changed: from a Modernist technocrat serving the state, he became the manager of scarce resources and individual talents, working alongside his parishioner clientele. The construction process also changed. Instead of a prefabricated

Source: Maciej Lulko / Architecture of the VII Day

Mary, Queen of Peace Catholic Church

building churned out of a factory, each church was slowly built as parishioners donated their labour on Saturdays and small sums of money on Sundays. As it was built, each church became imbued with its own community history, its own local myth.

Following the election of John Paul II – a Pole – to the papacy in 1978, and the rise of the Solidarity movement in 1980, the construction of churches became as much an expression of faith as it was a form of protest against the Communists. In particular, Solidarity triggered a wave of church building; hoping to maintain their hold on power, the government ignored the hundreds of new construction projects. The fantastic church designs were ruptures in the rigid state urbanism, a testament to the creative will of the people that built them.

In central and southern Poland, Architecture of the VII Day appeared immediately after the war – new structures started emerging from the ruins as soon as 1945. In western Poland it was different. Until the 1970s there was no official church administration which would run these projects. The construction of the Church of the Holy Spirit – the first one to appear in Wrocław – started only in 1973 and was finished in 1994. An avant-garde temple is imbued with a fascinating story of countless projects, proposed for the parish since the Thaw of 1956 and of a long community-driven construction. Another landmark of Architecture of the VII Day is the Mary, Queen of Peace Catholic Church, erected in the Popowice housing estate. The building permit for this temple was issued just after the Solidarity strikes in 1980. The building was designed by a group of thirty-year-old architects. The construction, in turn, was supervised by old masters drawing on pre-war masonry techniques. This unexpected collaboration bred one of the most original brick structures in Wrocław, where avant-garde ideas of the young architects interweave with the craft of the experienced masons.

Since the 1970s, around two dozen churches have been erected in Wrocław. Mostly they are located far from the centre in remote housing estates and suburbs. Due to the Socialist state's anti-religious policy, rather than being visually exposed they are hidden behind high concrete slabs of dwellings. That doesn't make Architecture of the VII Day less interesting – both the buildings and stories of their construction are gems worth discovering.

The Christ the Saviour Church was built between 1996 and 2001 by Jadwiga Grabowska-Hawrylak and Edmund Frąckiewicz.

Source: Igor Snopek / Architecture of the VII Day

Main Post Office (078)

St. Mary Magdalene Cathedral (010)

Hotel Mercure Panorama (124)

Old Town Hall (004)

Kameleon Department Store (066)

Hansel and Gretel (007)

Panoramic view of the medieval Market Square

Szewska Multi-functional Car Park (115)

St. Stanislaus, Dorothy and Vaclav Church (009)

Source: iStock (greir)

The main building of the University of Wrocław is located next to the tranquil banks of the River Oder

University of Wrocław (020)
Wyspa Słodowa

The Southern Hydroelectric Power Plant is situated where water mills used to stand

Southern Hydroelectric Power Plant (079)

Marina (146)

Northern Hydroelectric Power Plant (080)

Photo: Masako Tomokiyo

The skyline of Wrocław is dominated by Gothic churches and towering residential buildings

Source: iStock (Mariusz Szczygiel)

1200–1850
1850–1945
1945–1989
1990–2015

Photo: Bartek Barczyk

St. Giles Church

Katedralny Square
1220s

001 B

The Late Romanesque St. Giles Church is not only the oldest church in the city, but also the oldest preserved building there. Erected at the request of Wiktor, the Dean of the Wrocław Cathedral Chapter, the temple was probably built on the debris of an older structure. One of its Romanesque portals has been preserved up to the present day, while the second one is rooted in the Renaissance. The St. Giles Church is an example of a typical medieval single-pillar structure – the vault of the church rests on a single pillar and the brick arcade links the temple to the Late Gothic Chapter from the sixteenth century, forming the so-called Brama Kluskowa gate. The Chapter houses extensive collections of the Archiepiscopal Museum. The church survived the war, and thus became an important religious complex for Poles arriving in the Recovered Territories, resettled from the eastern regions. After the war, the building was cleared of its Baroque influences, external plasters were forged off, the double chancel arch was reconstructed, leaving however the flèche. The St. Giles Church was probably first constructed as a grave chapel for a Prince of Opole and Jarosław Opolski, the Bishop of Wrocław. Visiting the temple, we can marvel at the restored eighteenth-century Christ and Heavenly Mother statues.

Photo: iStock (E. Fesenko)

Photo: Bartek Barczyk

Photo: Philipp Meuser

Piast Dynasty Castle Relics 002 B
12 Świętego Marcina Street
12th–13th centuries

Few people know that the underground of the monastic house on Świętego Marcina Street houses the remains of the Piast dynasty castle relics, deposited approximately 4 m below ground level. The tenement belonging to the Congregation of the School Sisters of Notre Dame, constructed as of 1833, was initially erected as a school for girls. The building located at the back of the plot was erected on a former canonical curia, built in the fourteenth century on the walls of the former castle. The castle stretched to both sides of the current Marcina Street, linking the then water gate of the palace with its city wall. The castle lost its primary meaning and became a sacral structure as a result of the grand city development project on the left bank of the Odra River which took place after the Mongolian invasion of 1241. The castle comprises a palace linked to a Gothic court chapel. Their place is currently occupied by the monastic house. Completed in 1856, the building was reconstructed several times. A neo-Gothic wing was added in 1891 and in 1921, the neo-Romanesque front portal was erected. The site has been undergoing comprehensive preparations for the opening of the Piast Centre encompassing a culture centre and providing numerous attractions on the map of Lower Silesian historical sites.

Photo: Piast Centre

Photo: Bartek Barczyk

St. Martin Church

003 B

67 Świętego Marcina Street
Master Wiland
13th century, Tadeusz Kozaczewski and Edmund Małachowicz (restoration: 1957–1960)

Erected in the 1280s on the debris of a Romanesque court chapel, this masonry Gothic church designed by Wiland, the master of masonry, is the second oldest sacral building in Wrocław. The church is all that remains of a castle founded by dukes of the Piast dynasty. Established by Prince Henry IV Probus as a cloistral church devoted to Mary, Mother of God, the temple comprised a charnel house, i.e. a two-storey burial vault, the upper part of which served for conducting ceremonies, whereas the lower part served as a tomb. However, due to the simultaneous construction of the St. Cross Church, the works were suspended and completed in altered form in the fifteenth century. The church was consumed by fire twice (1466, 1544), whereas in 1571 it underwent complete restoration. Initially, the floor plan of the building consisted of a rectangular presbytery and an adjoining western octagonal aisle. However, after the final change of governing assumptions and after simplifying the structure, the buttresses were demolished; the northern wall of the presbytery was shifted to the north and the aisle was widened. The upper storey, devoid of vaults, was crowned with a painted coffer ceiling ornamented with stars. Destroyed in the turmoil of World War II, the church was reconstructed from 1957 to 1960. Reconstruction works were supervised by Tadeusz Kozaczewski and Edmund Małachowicz. By reducing a part of the aisle to the size of the original floor plan, as well as creating a superstructure and covering it with a canopy, the temple recovered its initial properties. After restoring the outline of the buttresses and position of the new floor in the southern part of the former castle area, the John XXIII monument designed by Ludwika Nitschowa was revealed in 1968. The interior includes a unique ten-segment Gothic architectural feature made from stone running along the presbytery.

Photo: Philipp Meuser

Photo: Philipp Meuser

Old Town Hall
Rynek – Ratusz 1
13th–16th centuries

004 B

Situated in the southeastern corner of the central market square development block, the Late Gothic City Hall building is one of the best-preserved buildings of this type in Poland. The two-storey building with three naves was erected on the floor plan of an extended rectangle, with a square tower and a rectangular Council and Jury building annex adjoining the northern façade. This unique example of lay Gothic architecture was built for nearly 250 years (between the thirteenth and sixteenth centuries). Since the beginning, it has served as a residence to city authorities and the judiciary. The final shape of the building was formed by the reconstruction between 1470 and 1480. The building was enlarged almost by half, adding several new rooms to the south and giving the entire structure a representative character by adding richly ornamented bay windows and roofs crowned with decorative tips. In 1510, the façade of the building was plastered and ornamented with paintings. In 1559, the town hall tower was elevated and covered by a Renaissance cupola. In turn, in 1580 an ornamental clock was installed in the eastern façade of the building. At the beginning of the nineteenth century, the councilmen transferred to the New Town Hall built nearby. Damaged during World War II, the building was reconstructed and restored afterwards.

Solny Square ↑
Solny Square
1242

005 B

Adjoining the southwestern corner of the Old Market Square, this square yard, which once served as a trading centre for salt imported from the Małopolska region (from Wieliczka and Halicz), is a flower market today. The square was probably built in 1242, when the city was replanned after the Mongolian invasion. During the Middle Ages, the square was referred to as the Polish Market and constituted a meeting spot for gold miners called *Walończycy*. In 1827, its name was changed to Blücherplatz, after the name of Field Marshal Blücher, whose monument was placed in the square. After World War II, the square received a historical name and the monument base was demolished. The space of the square is non-developed, and half of the frontal side is occupied by the Classicist Old Market building of 1822 as well as three historicising tenements. The eastern side of the square features, among other things, a store dating to the beginning of the twentieth century. The northern wall consists of a high-rise designed by Heinrich Rump, erected between 1930 and 1932 (currently the residence of the *Gazeta Wyborcza* journal), reconstructed in 1928 by Adolf Rading to lend a more Modernist touch. The square also features two tenements, including the fully preserved Oppenheim-family Baroque tenement from the middle of the eighteenth century. Destroyed during the war, the tenements were reconstructed between 1960 and 1961 with the objective to restore their Baroque look. In 1997, a spire designed by Adam Wyspiański, referring to the spire erected in 1948 next to the Centennial Hall, was placed at the centre of the square. Not everyone knows that a nearly 1,000 m^2 shelter capable of housing up to 300 people is situated beneath part of Solny Square.

Stare Jatki ↘

006 B

Malarska
14th century

Jatki, or portable market stands used for trading meat, are placed in rows along the narrow Malarska pedestrian street, constituting one of the most important elements of the old Wrocław urban landscape. At the beginning of the fourteenth century, the first wooden single-storey stands were transformed into narrow brick tenements, with the stands situated on the ground floor. In 1880, when the activity of the guild was restored, the stands started to serve their primary function again. The appearance and interior design of the buildings was standardised, among other things, by assimilating the size of the windows and doors. During the war, nearly half of the stands were destroyed and only twelve buildings were preserved. In 1951, the site was dedicated to new residential development. Building interiors were connected by shared staircases. In turn, the ground floors were transformed again into stands, in which part of the historical ceilings have been preserved. In 1992, part of the lower storeys were acquired by the Wrocław division of the Association of Polish Visual Artists, which founded, among other things, a musical club, a gallery and a handicraft shop on Malarska Street. In 1997, at the initiative of Piotr Wieczorek, a culture animator, a monument commemorating slaughtered animals was unveiled.

All photos: Philipp Meuser

Photo: Philipp Meuser

Hansel and Gretel

007 B

1 Świętego Mikołaja St., 39/40 Odrzańska St.
15th century, Christoph Hackner (reconstruction: 1954)

The northwestern corner of the Market Square is occupied by two tenements linked with an arcade. These belong to a larger group of houses belonging to the altarists of the St. Elizabeth Church, built around the church cemetery abandoned in the nineteenth century. The majority of these houses were also demolished in the middle of the nineteenth century, leaving only two of these which are connected by the former cemetery gate. All of the buildings feature a gothic structure with both Renaissance and Baroque elements. These masonry and plastered houses were covered with gable roofs. Their interiors feature wooden ceilings. The lower three-storey tenement situated on Swiętego Mikołaja Street – Hansel – is characterised by a smooth façade ornamented with simple window and door frames made from sandstone. A partially reconstructed portal, found in 1994, was built into the eastern part of the building. The façade is further decorated by the works of Eugeniusz Get Stankiewicz, a renowned copper engraver, who lived in this building until his death in 2011. The second tenement – the four-storey Gretel – was thoroughly reconstructed in 1954. The only parts preserved until today are the two levels of basements with barrel vaults from the fourteenth century. The gate linking the tenements was reconstructed to its Baroque form from 1728 according to a design by Christoph Hackner. In 1740, the buildings were restored again to reflect the Baroque style. After the war, the buildings were reconstructed twice (1959–1960 and 1972–1975) according to designs by the architect Emil Kaliski. Since the 1960s, the buildings have been owned by the Wrocław Enthusiasts Association which decided to place its offices there. The names reflecting the protagonists of the Grimm Brothers' fables were given by settlers arriving in Wrocław after World War II.

Photo: Bartek Barczyk

John the Baptist Archiepiscopal See

008 B

18 Katedralny Square
13th–14th centuries

Located in the oldest district of Wrocław, Ostrów Tumski, the Archiepiscopal See dating back to the thirteenth and fourteenth centuries is recognised as the first Gothic temple on Polish soil. The Gothic basilica, surrounded by multiple galilees and chapels from the outside, consists of a three-aisle, six-span choir, surrounded by a rectangular passage with two towers in the eastern corners, and a six-span body with two towers from the west. The temple was reconstructed many times. Successive works were supervised by Günter Grundmann, Joseph Ebers and Karl Lüdecke. Further on, the Bishop of Wrocław, Franciszek Ludwik Neuburg, founded the Elector's Chapel devoted to the Body of Christ, which was built between the years 1716 and 1724. During World War II, the Archiepiscopal See was destroyed to a large extent. The second stage of conservation works commenced in 1968 – the roofing and the chapels were reconstructed. On 14 August 1991, the cathedral towers received their copulas. An elevator was installed in the north-western tower, which allows for access to the viewpoint around the copula. The interior of the temple includes, among other things, a Late Gothic pentaptych from Lublin, stalls from the St. Vincent Cathedral and the preserved part of the tube organs from the Centennial Hall.

Photo: iStock (Krzysztof Nahlik)

Source: iStock (efesenko)

St. Stanislaus, Dorothy and Vaclav Church
3 Wolności Square
1351–1686

009 B

The church was built to commemorate the agreement between Casimir the Great and Charles IV, regarding the rights to Silesia. Construction works commenced in 1351. The three-aisle tall hall with the five-span presbytery featuring a pentagonal apse, crowned with a cross vault, was built first. The presbytery was only completed in 1381. In 1401, the completed main aisle was crowned with a star vault, and the side aisles with shifting vaults. The presbytery and the aisles were covered with steep roofs. The side aisles were terminated with towers adjoining the presbytery, which however did not exceed the height of the main roof – the northern tower remained unfinished. Entrances were positioned in the side aisles. The western façade was crowned with an ornamental ceramic tip with pinnacles. To the south, the church adjoined the cloister development. In 1686, the cloister buildings and the interior of the church were renovated to reflect the Baroque style. Since 1810, the cloister buildings fulfilled various functions, i.e. served as a prison. Ultimately, at the end of the nineteenth century these were demolished. It was then that a new entrance to the church, including a neo-Gothic portal, was forged. The church survived the war in a relatively good condition and is still considered one of the best preserved medieval monuments in Wrocław. Visitors to the church can marvel at the main altar with the *St. Dorothy Martyrdom* painting, the John the Baptist statue and the St. John the Evangelist's statue sculpted by Georg Leonard Weber. The coats of arms of Poland, the Czech Republic and the Swidnica Principality were engraved in the wall of the presbytery from the side of Świdnicka Street to commemorate the 1351 meeting of the monarchs.

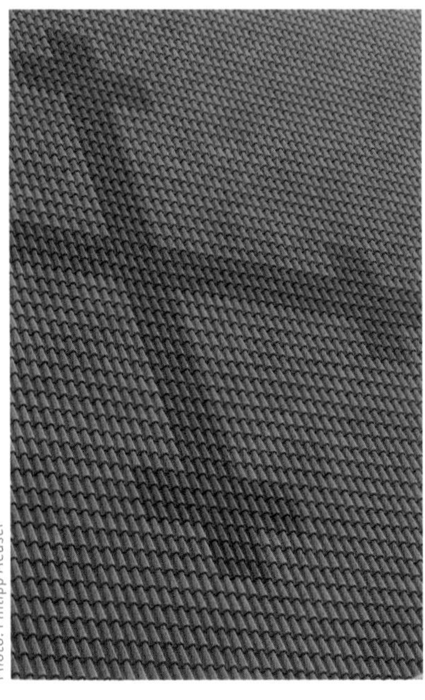
Photo: Philipp Meuser

Source: iStock (CCat82)

St. Mary Magdalene Cathedral 010 B
10 Szewska Street
1342–1362,
Copulas and towers: 15th century

The area where the construction of the St. Mary Magdalene Church commenced in 1342 had been previously occupied by numerous Christian temples. In the eleventh century, a church was built there and then destroyed during the Mongolian invasion of 1241. The next temple, erected in the Romanesque-Gothic style between 1242 and 1248, was consumed by fire on 8 May 1342, providing a site for the much larger, Late Gothic St. Mary Magdalene Church (built between 1342 and 1362, and which survived nearly untouched until the outburst of World War II). This transept-free temple has a six-span aisle and a straight enclosed presbytery without an ambulatory. To the north, the presbytery is adjoined by a two-storey sacristy. The aisles have cross-ribbed vaults and the presbytery is crowned with a star vault. In turn, the extended side aisles have triple vaults. The buttress arches are located above the side aisle roofs. The towers were completed in the middle of the fifteenth century. The fifteenth century also marks the period in which the Bridge of the Witches (which used to connect them) is first mentioned. In 1481, the sheet metal (copper) copulas were finished. In the fifteenth and sixteenth centuries, several chapels were built around the church. St. Maria Magdalena Church was the first in Silesia to receive an evangelical sermon from Johann Heß in 1523. On 23 March 1887, during the celebration of Emperor Wilhelm I's birthday, a fire caused by fireworks consumed the northern tower. Furthermore, the temple underwent considerable damage during the last days of World War II. Between 1960 and 1970, it underwent thorough reconstruction, after which the church stunned with its Renaissance pulpit from the end of the sixteenth century, and the Romanesque Ołbin Portal of the twelfth century, transferred from the Benedictine Abbey, among other things.

Photo: Masako Tomokiyo

Source: iStock (karp85)

St. Cross Church

011 B

Kościelny Square
Master Wiland
Presbytery: 1288–1295,
Aisle and transept: 1320–1350,
Towers: 1484

It was 1288 when the construction of the church founded by Prince Henry IV Probus began. The temple was to become a symbol of the magnificence of the ruler governing in the period of regional division. It was his ambition to reunite the Polish lands under his rule. This tall temple with its own chapter continues to provide an impressive experience. Completed in the year 1484, the church comprises a two-level masonry Gothic temple, erected on a Latin cross floor plan. The four-span extended presbytery is terminated by a trilateral ambulatory. The transept with the same number of vaults was terminated in the same manner. The three aisles create a hall. The lower storey has one cross-ribbed vault, while the second storey introduces double-length vaults in the central aisle. In turn, the side aisles feature stunning triple vaults. The corners between the hall and the transept feature two towers – whereas only the southern one was completely finished. The church features an atypical two-storey interior layout, in which both the upper and the lower temple reproduce the floor plan in a nearly identical manner. The central aisle and the presbytery have a shared, longitudinal, tall roof, whereas the side aisles have crosswise gable roofs. After it was demolished by the Swedish army in the course of the Thirty Years' War, the church regained its Baroque interior during the seventeenth century. The temple suffered as a result of the city siege of 1945, but was restored between 1946 and 1956.

St. Corpus Christi

012 B

Bożego Ciała 1
First half of the 15th century

This Gothic masonry temple, one of the most important elements of the city's defense fortification system, was erected in the fifteenth century, although, according to some historical sources, the first church to be built on this site originated in the fourteenth century. Thanks to the efforts of its churchgoers, the renovation and reconstruction of the church started in 1700. As a result, the church gained its Baroque splendour. In June 1749, as a result of the explosion of one of the gunpowder towers, the building was severely damaged. During the Seven Years' War and the Napoleon Wars, the temple was further vandalised. A general renovation of the church was initiated in 1810. During the same year, the church was given over to the Prussian state. At the beginning of the twentieth century, the temple was recovered by the Catholic Church and underwent a thorough renovation in the 1920s and 1930s. This Gothic basilica temple has one of the largest aisles among all of the churches in Wrocław. The main aisle without a spatially separated presbytery is a five-span and trilaterally enclosed structure, whereas the side aisles are enclosed by perpendicular walls. The western façade is ornamented with a sharp arched window and a ceramic tip with pinnacles and panels. This simple temple has never had a tower, which probably results from the observance of the Knight Order of Saint John praising poverty and modesty. The church was completely ruined in the course of the battle of Wrocław and its interior consumed by fire. The reconstruction process was initiated in 1956 and conducted until 1977.

Photo: Philipp Meuser

Church of St. John Nepomucene 013 C

Dąbska Alley
ca. 1575

The small church of St. John Nepomucene made of larch wood is situated within Szczytnicki Park. This unique monument from the second half of the sixteenth century (approximately 1575) was brought to Wrocław in 1913 for the Centennial Exhibition presenting the history of Silesia. Erected in Stare Koźle in Upper Silesia, the church was initially transferred to Kędzierzyn, from where it was transported to the Cemetery Art Exhibition. The reconstruction of the church in Szczytnicki Park was supervised by Theo Effenberger, a Wrocław-based architect. Its interiors were renovated by the students of the Wrocław Academy of Fine Arts, supervised by Fryderyk Pautsch. The building features a log structure and its roof is shingled. The temple consists of a square aisle and a trilaterally enclosed presbytery, as well as a low tower with a galilee. Unfortunately, the original eighteenth-century furnishing of the church, including the stained glass windows, did not survive World War II. The Church of St. John Nepomucene came into the spotlight when, at the end of the 1950s, some of the missing paintings by Matejko, Kossak and Gierymski were found there, hidden from sight. Since the 1970s, the church is administered voluntarily by the Wrocław-Fabryczna division of the Polish Tourist Association.

Psie Budy

014 B

Psie Budy
15th century

Those who want to feel the true climate of the medieval city, the tight development and picturesque streets (though somewhat faded with the lapse of time) must certainly visit Psie Budy. The development of this part of the city was erected in the fourteenth century and the first houses were lined just outside the city walls between the wall and the internal moat referred to as Czarna Oława. The alley behind the streets Ruska and Koński Targ (today's Karola Szajnochy Street) bore different names in the fifteenth century, such as Hundhäuser (Hound's Houses) and Hinterhäuser (Rear Houses). At the beginning of the nineteenth century, one of the oldest water mills in the city, which was built in 1291 and situated in the area of today's Bohaterów Getta Square linking Psie Budy to Szajnochy Street, was demolished. At the beginning of the twentieth century, the street was named after a Wrocław merchant and social activist, Johan Georg Krull. Unfortunately, the majority of the development was destroyed during the war. It was to be reconstructed only in part. Reconstruction works were managed by Stanisław Koziczuk between 1958 and 1961. However, the reconstruction process was chaotic and random and did not take any historical models into account. In the 1970s, the east-west route was built along Czarna Oława. What survived from the old district was Szajnochy Street and its extension: Psie Budy. And although, from an architectural point of view, only few development elements display any historical value, Psie Budy is definitely a place worth visiting.

All photos: Philipp Meuser

City Arsenal
9 Antoniego Cieszyńskiego Street
1459

015 B

In the year 1491, fearing an attack from the Czech King George of Poděbrady, the city authorities decided to build an arsenal in the vicinity of the Mikołajska Gate. The building, or rather its southern wing, was initially to serve as a granary. At the beginning of the sixteenth century, the weaponry depot was transferred to the building, which has been referred to as the *Zeughaus* since then. The northern wing was erected in 1490. In turn, the western wing was built as late as 1570. The arsenal yard was enclosed by the eastern wing, built in 1658. The building also includes two towers. The northern tower, a remnant of the fourteenth-century second line of defence walls, is 20.5 m tall. The second one is 13 m tall. The area between the granary and the fourteenth-century walls was filled with successive structures, such as a coach house, a smithy and a gunsmithing workshop. Currently, the city arsenal has a tetragon floor plan, including a central yard. The simple and crude form of the arsenal houses a rare woodwork structure referring to traditional Silesian granaries. This perfectly preserved complex is the site of numerous artistic events. The building houses the Military Museum, the Architecture Museum Archives and the Museum of Archaeology.

Former City Prison

016 B

6 Więzienna Street
14th–16th centuries

The number of convicts grew with the dynamic development of the city. At some point, their number surpassed the capacity of the city hall dungeons. Therefore, in the middle of the fourteenth century, the city government launched the construction of the city prison. The first structure of the complex was the square tower reflecting the style of castle towers. Successive buildings were gradually added throughout the years. Ultimately, in the 1680s, the complex took the form of an enclosed tetragon with an internal yard. Prisoners were kept in the basements of the northern wing. In turn, the dungeons of the eastern part were dedicated to interrogations, often with the use of horrific persuasion tools. The city prison was primarily devoted to incarcerate lower-level inmates, whereas the higher-rank residents were kept in the City Hall tower. Rumour has it that the renowned sculptor Wit Stwosz was to serve a one-year sentence in this prison for forging a bill of exchange. At the turn of the eighteenth and nineteenth centuries, the building ceased to serve as a prison. Instead, the complex housed a pawnshop whose vault was protected by the armoured door found in one of the rooms today. The building survived the war in very good condition. From 1967 to 1973, it underwent a general renovation, thanks to which we can still marvel at the wooden porches and historical interiors from various epochs, including the Baroque wooden ceilings covered with seventeenth-century polychromies. The building currently houses the Faculty of Archaeology and Ethnology of the Polish Academy of Sciences.

All photos: Philipp Meuser

Architecture Museum

017 B

5 Bernardyńska
Hans Berthold (1517), Edmund Małachowicz (1961-1965), ARCH_IT (reconstruction: 2014)

In 1965, Poland's first and only architecture museum was opened in the interior of the reconstructed fifteenth-century Bernardine Order. The complex comprises the St. Bernard of Siena Church and a cloister tetragon surrounding a picturesque internal square yard. Initially a branch of the Museum of the City of Wrocław, the museum has been operating as an independent unit since 1971. The history of this place extends back to 1453, when St. John of Capistrano, the General Inquisitor of Pope Nicolaus V and the founder of the Bernardine Order, arrived in Wrocław. Soon after he received the site from the authorities, he built a wooden church here. Ten years later, the wooden structure was replaced by a masonry church, which can be visited today, surrounded by a cloister development. Construction works were supervised by Hans Berthold of Łużyce and construction was completed in 1517. In 1522, when the Order left the city, the cloister complex was transformed into a city hospital, and the church was handed over to the evangelical community. At the end of World War II, the cloister was bombarded and then reconstructed from 1956 to 1974. It was then that the complex was adapted for museum purposes. The layout remained unchanged. The museum is the venue for numerous concerts, theatre performances and a One Project Gallery, which presents the most interesting architectural projects implemented in Poland. Visitors can marvel at, among other things, the exquisite collection of stained glass, including a stained glass window from the turn of the twelfth and thirteenth centuries, the oldest preserved specimen of this kind in the Polish lands.

The Bear Tower

018 B

8 Plac bpa Nankiera

13th century, Mirosław Przyłęcki (reconstruction: 1957–1958)

A hidden medieval tower, one of the oldest elements of the city's defence fortification system, is located at the back of the market hall on Nankiera Street, in the yard of the blocks of flats situated on Piaskowa Street. The walls were erected in the middle of the thirteenth century, after the Mongolian invasion of 1241. The tower was part of this very first defence development which was initially built as a rectangular bay. In the first half of the fourteenth century, the complex was raised by one storey, enclosed from the side of the city and covered with a hip roof featuring a short ridge. The tower survived in this shape until World War II. With time, the facility lost its military function, thanks to which it was salvaged from the demolition order issued by the Napoleon army in 1807. During the siege of the Breslau stronghold, the tower was predominantly destroyed. However, after the war, as part of a reconstruction process encompassing all structures certifying the Piast dynasty origins of the city, the complex was rebuilt according to a design by Mirosław Przyłęcki. In the course of reconstruction, the lion statue found in the vicinity of Łaciarska Street, resembling a bear to some, was in-built in the eastern corner of the tower. Hence the name: the Bear Tower.

All photos: Philipp Meuser

Photo: Philipp Meuser

Bastion Ceglarski – Wzgórze Polskie

019 B

52 Purkyniego Street
Hans Schneider von Lindau
1585

In the fourteenth century, some of the city's defence fortifications were located in the vicinity of the Ceglarska Gate. However, the bastion in its current shape was erected in 1585 during the reconstruction of the defence walls, according to a design by a recognised architect, Hans Schindler von Lindau, who specialised in defence development. The bastion had a masonry casemate. With time, a small corner vantage tower, and a ravelin – a protruding, triangular fortification element – were added to the complex, which survived in this form until the 1807 demolition of the city walls, when the casemate was buried and the area with the bastion was transformed into a viewpoint. This place was one of the favourite spots of Karl von Holtei, a Silesian poet of the Romantic period. Following his death in 1880, a monument sculpted by Albert Rachner, a Wrocław-based artist, was erected on this site and was named the Holei Heights. During the siege of Wrocław, a military hospital was set up underground. After the war, the name of the hill was changed to Wzgórze Polskie (Polish Heights – from the medieval Polska Street, or Polnischegasse). In 1970, the bastion was recorded in the register of monuments, and conservation works commenced two years later. In turn, in the 1980s, the site was drained and the complex was set to be thoroughly reconstructed. Unfortunately, these efforts were never implemented.

Photo: Philipp Meuser

Source: iStock (Gosiek-B)

University of Wrocław 020 B
1 Uniwersytecki Square
Johann Blasius Peintner,
Joseph Frisch (western wing: 1728–1736, eastern wing: 1734–1740)

The history of the University of Wrocław, brought into life on 1 October 1702 at the request of Emperor Leopold I Habsburg, was rather stormy. The first works on the edifice commenced in April 1728, although its plans had been prepared two years earlier. The construction process, supervised by architect Peintner, was initially quite efficient. At the end of 1729, when the walls were completed, the constructor proceeded to the vaults and in 1730 to the roof structure. Unfortunately, due to the shortage of funds, all works were nearly completely withheld by that time. Although John Christoph Hanke was working on the frescos in the famous Leopold Hall, the Mathematical Tower was still under construction. The western wing was finally completed in 1738, when the statues of Four Cardinal Virtues were placed on the portico balustrade. After Peintner's death, all supervision works were taken over by Joseph Frisch. In 1732, he ordered the demolition of old developments to make room for the eastern wing. However, a sudden flood interrupted the works which ultimately ended in 1740. Unfortunately, a year later, when Silesia was occupied by the army of Frederic II, the building was intended for a field hospital. Excluded from use, the Leopold Hall was salvaged from destruction. The University returned to its activities in 1763. At the end of the eighteenth century, a series of rather unfortunate renovations was conducted. In 1811, the academic year was officially opened in the building by Viadrina University, transferred from Frankfurt (Oder). Afterwards, the building would undergo numerous renovations, which, unfortunately, were not always conducted with due care and consideration for the architectural details of this Baroque edifice.

Photo: Thomas Michael Krüger

Leopold Hall
1 Uniwersytecki Square
Christophorus Tausch,
Johann Handke
1728–1732

021 B

This magnificent Late Baroque hall, serving as one of the most representative rooms of the main University building, is a priceless lay monument of its time. The author of the design of the hall (named after the founder of the University of Wrocław) was the student of the renowned Italian architect Andrea Pozza, namely Christophorus Tausch. The tripartite interior, built on the plant of an extended trapezoid, was created through separation of the podium auditorium and music

Source: iStock (Angelo D'Amico)

gallery resting on pillars. The author of the frescos was Johann Handke of Olomouc and the statues were sculpted by the Moravian artist Franz Joseph Mangoldt, whereas the ornaments were the work of the master Ignazio Provisore. The richly ornamented interior of the hall houses numerous exquisite examples of virtuosity from artists and craftsmen of that time. One of the most interesting works is the polychromy presenting the allegorical image of Silesia, located above the gallery. In the polychromy, Silesia is sitting on a throne, sided by the personifications of Odra and Wrocław. The hall, which continues to this day to hold the important academic events, has survived all wars nearly unchanged.

Source: iStock (PM78)

University Church
1 Uniwersytecki Square
Teodor Moretti
1706

022 B

One of the most stunning Baroque temples in Wrocław was built on the original site of the southeastern part of the imperial castle, with its only remains in the form of the one-storey Renaissance building used as a sacristy. The University Church is a typical example of a single-aisle Jesuit temple, with two rows of side chapels topped with galleries opening to the aisles. The building was designed by the Italian architect Teodor Moretti, and Mateusz Biener and Jan Knoll were put in charge of construction works. The project was completed in 1706, when Johann Michael Rottmayer von Rosenbrunn completed his cycle of illusionistic frescos decorating the walls and the vault of the temple. From 1722 to 1734, Christoph Tausch created the final Late Baroque style of the interior by designing, among other things, the Passion altar in the Lady of Sorrows Chapel (completed in 1725) and the monumental main altar (completed in 1726). Several of the sculptures were created by Franz Joseph Mangoldt, whereas the two richly ornamented confessionals are the work of the sculpting master Siegwitz. Despite numerous political whirlwinds, the church has survived up to the present day in very good condition. It has not incurred any significant damages, even during the siege of Wrocław of 1945. Thanks to this, the building endured, untouched. Inside, visitors can marvel at the unique marble copy of Michelangelo's *Pieta*.

Source: iStock (PM78)

Source: iStock (Tomeyk)

Ossolińscy State Company

023 B

37 Szewska Street
Johann Chrysostom Neborak
1690–1710

The site intended for the construction of the Order of the Brothers Hospitallers was granted to the state in the thirteenth century by the widow of Henry II the Pious. The Knights of the Cross with the Red Star, devoted to helping the poor, took over the adjoining St. Matthias Church. Unfortunately, the medieval developments have not survived. At the turn of the seventeenth and eighteenth centuries, these were replaced with Baroque structures designed by Johann Chrystostom Neborak. Apart from a hospital, the cloister also included a dormitory for impoverished students and the pupils of the Jesuit academy. From the beginning of the nineteenth century until the outburst of World War II, the building also housed a Catholic St. Matthias gymnasium. The complex was reconstructed from 1910 to 1911, and part of the buildings were demolished. After the war, a series of renovation works was performed; however, it was not until the turn of the twentieth and twenty-first centuries that the complex received a comprehensive renovation. The copula destroyed during the war was restored and the Baroque yard returned to its original splendour. Since 1947, the building has housed the Ossolińscy State Company which stores the most valuable national collections, including the manuscript of *Pan Tadeusz* by Adam Mickiewicz.

Royal Palace (The Museum of the City of Wrocław) ↗→

024 B

35 Kazimierza Wielkiego Street
Johann Boumann (extension: 1753), Carl Gotthard Langhans (extension: 1797)

The history of this palace situated in the southern part of the Old Town extends back to the year 1717, when a small residence styled according to the Viennese Baroque, located on Kazimierza Wielkiego Street, was purchased and reconstructed by Baron Heinrich Gottfried Spaetgen. In 1750, following the Baron's death, the residence was purchased by Frederic II the Great, the new ruler of Silesia. At his request, the royal architect, Johann Boumann, reconstructed the palace, adding a two-storey Rococo wing on the side of the garden. The new wing housed a music room, an office and a library. In the 1790s, the oldest part of the palace was reconstructed to reflect the Classicist style, additionally enclosing the yard with two one-storey guardhouses with an entry gate in the middle. The works were supervised by architect Carl Gotthard Langhans. In the middle of the nineteenth century, at the request of Frederic William IV, the Berlin architect Friedrich August Stuhler extended the palace considerably, giving it a truly royal character. It was then that the new southern wing reflecting the Florence Renaissance style was erected. The northern yard was enriched with two impressive, three-storey wings (eastern and western) which were connected to

Photo: Philipp Meuser

a colonnade with entrance gates (1867). After World War I, the building was dedicated to museum purposes. At the end of World War II, the complex was severely destroyed. Only the oldest part of the palace, the northern wing, and a fragment of the southern wing, which were reconstructed in the 1960s, have been preserved today. In 2009, following a thorough renovation, the palace became the residence of the Museum of the City of Wrocław.

Source: iStock (Hermsdorf)

Divine Providence Church ↘ 025 B

29 Kazimierza Wielkiego Street
Johann Boumann Senior, Friedrich Arnold
1746–1750

The construction of this evangelical church – also referred to as the court church, and designed by the royal architect Boumann Senior in cooperation with Friedrch Arnold – was initiated in 1746. Unfortunately, the nearly finished building was consumed in whole by fire in 1749. The temple was consecrated on 27 October 1750. The Late Baroque church with a singular aisle is roofed with a spherical vault. The rectangular room is filled with two gallery storeys, outlining the oval aisle. The five-storey tower with the clock is covered by a straight kiln roof shaped like a four-wall pyramid, crowned with a metal cross, protruding from the front line of the walls to create a hollow-corner avant-corps. The building surprises with the exceptional simplicity of its interiors. White walls and furnishing elements, as well as large windows in the temple, direct focus on the most important elements of the interior – the monumental altar's pulpit. Apart from this, the second showcase is the Rococo organ prospect situated on the second gallery level. The interior of the church was renovated a few times. The first thorough renovation was conducted in 1850, and the second one in 1928. The building was slightly damaged during the war. Renovations were performed in both 2000 and 2016.

Photo: Philipp Meuser

Source: iStock (Ireneusz Wojtowicz)

Cultural Centre of Leśnica Castle ↑

026 A

1 Świętojański Square
Christoph Hackner (1735–1740), Joseph Peter Lenné (park: 1836), Ludwik Grzybacz, Stefan Müller (reconstruction: 1958)
12th–18th centuries

The first residence of the Wrocław Principal Piast dynasty was built here at the beginning of the twelfth century. However, after the death of Henry VI in 1335, the Leśnica property was handed over to the Czech kings. After that, the castle would change ownership several times. The Hussite army destroyed the building in 1428. In turn, in 1494 Leśnica was purchased by the van Hörnig line. Count Heinrich von Hörnig commenced a thorough reconstruction of the building in 1610. Unfortunately, the Thirty Years' War left the castle in ruins. At the beginning of the eighteenth century, the castle was purchased by the von Forno family to undergo the next reconstruction. This Renaissance, three-storey building with a basement was erected on a 21 m long square floor plan, whereas four towers crowned with copulas were erected in the corners. The mansard roof was covered with roofing tiles. The tympanum façade is ornamented with a triangular tip with a window. The southbound main entrance is decorated by a cartouche with the coat of arms, placed above a small balcony. In the middle of the eighteenth century, the castle became the property of the Knights of the Cross with the Red Star, who changed the interiors, adding a Baroque character. The war turmoil spared the castle; even the remnants of the fortifications surrounding the complex were preserved, together with four towers and traces of a moat. Unfortunately, nearly none of the castle's furnishing elements have survived. From 1959 to 1963, the castle was adapted for the purposes of a culture centre. In 1972, it was recorded in the city of Wrocław register of monuments. Today, the castle houses the Castle Culture Centre.

Wrocław Opera House ↗

027 B

35 Świdnicka Street
Carl Ferdinand Langhans
1839–1841

On 13 October 1841, the Wrocław Opera House was officially opened with the premiere of Goethe's *Egmont*, featuring Beethoven's compositions. This classicist edifice, built according to a design by Carl Ferdinand Langhans and furnished with a state-of-the-art stage, would accommodate 1,600 spectators. The opening of the Opera House was a symbol of the cultural aspirations of the developing city of Wrocław, where the city theatre was operating. It was the Wrocław Opera House where the first German performance of *Boris Godunov* by Modest Mussorgsky took place, as well as the world premiere of *Eros and Psyche* by Ludomir Różycki. The opera house building designed by Langhans was consumed by fire twice (1865 and 1871). The first reconstruction was supervised

Photo: Bartek Barczyk

by K. Lüdecke – who elevated the auditorium and the fly, and added the paint shop pavilion. After the second fire, the building was reconstructed according to a design by Karl Schmidt, who ornamented the edges of the roof with sandstone sculptures of the muses. The building survived World War II in a relatively good condition. The only damaged elements were the muse sculptures. From 1954 to 1956, the southern part of the building was extended. In turn, from 1977 to 2006 the building was thoroughly upgraded. However, we can continue to marvel at the perfectly preserved, opulent nineteenth-century ornaments, such as the emperor's box and the plafond with the images of renowned composers.

White Stork Synagogue ↘ 028 B

7 Pawła Włodkowica Street
Carl Ferdinand Langhans
1827–1829

The idea for this Classicist synagogue was born in 1826. A year later, at the initiative of the First Brothers' Association, the construction of this neo-Classicist edifice designed by Carl Langhans, a renowned German architect, commenced. The interior of the temple was ornamented by the paintings of a Jewish artist: Raphael Biow. Opened in 1829, the temple was first used by a liberal faction of the Wrocław Jewish commune. After the New Synagogue was built in 1872, the building was taken over by conservative Jews, which resulted in its successive reconstructions. In 1905, the first significant reconstruction was conducted under the supervision of the Erlich brothers. It was then that the neo-Romanesque reinforced galleries for women were installed. In 1929, the building underwent thorough renovation, during which the interiors and façades were restored and electrical lighting and central heating were installed. On the Crystal Night, the Nazis destroyed the interior of the temple. In 1943, the German occupants transformed the synagogue into a warehouse for storing plundered Jewish property. Although the Jewish Committee in Wrocław took over the building in August 1945, successive emigration waves and recurring acts of vandalism contributed to the demise of the once magnificent edifice. Ultimately, after two fires, the building was handed over to the restored Jewish Commune in Wrocław in 1996 which commenced with the reconstruction of the building. Construction works were managed by Anna Kościuk. In May 2007, the Centre for Jewish Culture and Education opened in the building.

Photo: Philipp Meuser

Świebodzki Railway Station ↑ 029 B

Orląt Lwowskich Square
Alex Cochius (1842)
W. Kyllman, A. Heyden, K. Lüdecke (reconstruction: 1868–1874)

The Wrocław Świebodzki Railway Station is the oldest of three preserved railway stations in Wrocław. Erected in 1842, the station was created as the first stop on the Świebodzka line, electrified in 1914. Initially, the one-storey railway station building, featuring the two-storey central part situated on Tęczowa Street, had two platforms with a roof resting on slim columns. The turntable was located next to the area of today's Orląt Lwowskich Square. The second pavilion was erected to the north of the tracks. Between 1868 and 1874, the building was thoroughly reconstructed to acquire an impressive façade. It has survived in this shape until the present day. The Świebodzki Railway Station was put out of work in 1991. Since then, the complex has been leased, among others, by the Polish Theatre. The Swiebodzki Stage became an important spot on the cultural map of the city and the region. This was the site of the premieres of numerous performances by Jan Klata or Krystian Lupa.

Railway Directorate Building → 030 B

13 Joannitów Street
Hugo König
1911–1915

This four-storey building was erected on a rectangular floor plan with two yards, and covered with a gable roof with two levels of eyebrow attic windows. The impressive frontage facing the west is decorated with a Corinthian portico. The axis of the western façade is emphasised by six semi-columns preceding a shallow avant-corps, behind which a representative staircase is situated. The main entrance to the Royal Railway Directorate venue was ornamented by a bas-relief presenting the symbol of the railway: the winged wheel. The form of the entire building displays a clear reference to Baroque. The base and the rounded corners of the edifice are covered with bossage. Six sculptures presenting the Greek gods, serving as an allegory of Industry (Aphrodite), Mining (Hestia), Commerce (Hermes), Transport (Eos), the Military (Ares) and Agriculture (Demeter) by the renowned German sculptor Peter Breuer were placed above the mezzanine. The ornamental garden, which once adjoined the eastern façade, has now been replaced with a car park.

St. Joseph's Care Church → 031 A

1 Ołbińska Street
Carl Ferdinand Langhans
1821–1823

The first temple of the fifteenth century was located on the site of today's church by Carl Langhans. However, due to successive military operations, as well as fires and floods, the St. Ursula and the Eleven Hundred Virgins' Church was reconstructed multiple times. The building in its current shape was built from 1821 to 1823 according to a design by Karl Langhans, the renowned architect responsible for the Wrocław Opera House building, among other things. Initially, the building was to refer to the Roman Pantheon. The temple was erected on the floor plan of a dodecagon, covered with a kiln roof with a wide lantern and connected to a vestibule constituting the frontage with two towers. The interior of this Late Classicist building consists of a central hall with arcade galleries. The pulpit was placed in the centre to reflect the characteristic layout of a Protestant church. The façade of the church was maintained in the arcade style, whereas its details referred both to Romanesque and Gothic architecture. The façade of the church is ornamented by three Late Gothic fifteenth-century bas-reliefs by the master Briccius Gauske, transferred here from the dismantled Mikołajska Gate. The building suffered severe damage during World War II. In April 1946, it was handed over to Discalced Carmelites.

All photos: Philipp Meuser

1200–1850
1850–1945
1945–1989
1990–2015

Partisan Hill
Piotra Skargi/Nowa Street
Karol Schmidt
1866–1867

032 B

In 1866, at the request of Adolf Leibich, a financier and industrialist, works commenced to reconstruct the Pannier Hill erected according to a design by Johann Friedrich Knorr. The ambition of the initiator and the author of the design – Karl Schmidt – was to create a magnificent site accessible to all residents of the developing city. Completed in September 1867, the building comprised three levels. The lowest one, incorporated into the hill, served as an atrium with an interior accessed from the side of Sakwowa Street (the current Kołłątaja Street). The second level was a terrace surrounded by a colonnaded semi-circle, with two pavilions and a fountain in the centre. The third level, that is the roof of the colonnade, featured a three-level octagonal building with an extensive ground floor serving as a viewpoint. The statue of Victoria, sculpted by the Berlin sculptor Christian Daniel Rauch, was crowned with a helmet. This project also initiated the Wrocław New Renaissance trend. To honour the founder, the hill was named Liebichshöhe. Unfortunately, during the siege of the city, the building situated on the third level was completely destroyed. Right after the war, the Communist authorities destroyed part of the building's furnishing, including the monument by Daniel Friedrich Schleimacher, originating in 1869. The name of the hill was changed to Partisan Hill. Despite this, the site was still teeming with life. On 10 May 1967, a construction disaster took place, taking the life of one person. Since then, the building has fallen into demise. Despite the renovation commenced in 1974, it has never regained its full glory.

BWA Awangarda
31-32 Wita Stwosza Street
Carl Gotthard Langhans
1765–1773/1966

033 B

Between 1714 and 1722, a Baroque palace designed by Christoph Hackner was built in place of the former residence of the Brzeg and Oleśnica Piast dynasty. Unfortunately, the building burnt down in the course of the Seven Years' War. Construction of a new square according to a design by the princely construction inspector, Carl Gotthard Langhans, commenced in 1765. Within seven years, a three-storey edifice covering the entire quarter, with a mezzanine floor and an elegant façade reflecting outstanding Italian models, was erected. The building has since become one of the most stunning examples of Early Classicism in Wrocław. In 1802, the building was occupied by the city authorities. The palace was nearly completely destroyed during the siege of Wrocław. Right after the war, the relatively well-preserved ground floor was dismantled on the account of brick shortage. For many years, the ruins served as an excellent film location. In 1966, the living ruins were adapted for exhibition purposes, and an interesting combination of a Classicist palace with a Modernist pavilion was created. The Awangarda gallery was established and has been operating here since. In 2006, the gallery was renovated.

All photos: Philipp Meuser

Source: iStock (Kavalenkava Volha)

Wrocław Main Railway Station 034 B

105 Piłsudskiego Street
Wilhelm Grapow (1855–1857), Grupa 5 Architekci (renovation: 2010–2013)

The construction of the new main railway station building designed by Wilhelm Grapow commenced in 1855. Apart from the platforms, the building was also to house administrative offices. A 200 m long platform hall covered with a partially glazed roof was created and posed as one of the largest buildings of this type in Europe. The northern side of the hall was adjoined by a symmetrical railway station building styled after the English neo-Gothic resembling the Tudor epoch style. Soon afterwards, the needs surpassed the building's capacity, which had to be extended. The first extension was carried out at the turn of the nineteenth and twentieth centuries. Performed between 1899 and 1904 according to a design by Bernard Klüshe, the reconstruction outlined the preservation of a large part of the building's structure, and added quite a few Art Nouveau elements. In the process, the coal deposits located to the south of the railway station were eliminated, leaving room for five new platforms. Five parallel tunnels were also created as passageways under the railway embankment. During World War II, the German authorities decided to build concrete shelters under the yard in front of the station. Prior to 1949, nearly all war damages were repaired or removed. The building was renovated in 1960, and a part of its façade was reconstructed. Today's condition of the railway station and its environment is the result of a thorough revitalisation that was implemented from 2010 to 2013. The winning design by Grupa 4 Architekci was selected in an open competition.

Source: iStock (Paweł Szczepański)

Gwardia Sports Club

035 B

17 Krupnicza Street
Karl Johann Bogislaw Lüdecke
1867

The committee for the 1863 competition for the New Market building selected a neo-Gothic design, reflecting the English Tudor epoch style. The front façade of this masonry palace-castle building was ornamented by powerful lateral avant-corps crowned with towers. The ground floor arcades of the side façade were covered by a mock terrace. The building's rich ornaments include the allegorical sculptures presenting Commerce, Agriculture, Seafaring, Shepherding, Metallurgy and Mining. These were created by G. Michaelis and A. Kern. The building impressed with its richly ornamented market hall with Silesia's only coffer ceiling. The interiors of the building were reconstructed in 1928 according to Heinrich Lauterbach's design. As a result, the ornamental ceiling and a series of decorative elements were removed and the hall acquired an expressionist décor. The building survived World War II and was taken over by the Gwardia Sports Club in 1945, which has been its owner since. In turn, the main market hall was transformed into a sports hall.

Photos: Philipp Meuser

Grunwaldzki Bridge
Grunwaldzki Bridge
Robert Weyrauch, Martin Mayer
1908–1910

036 B

A competition for the construction of a new bridge on the River Odra to link the downtown with the northeastern part of the city was announced in the first decade of the twentieth century. The winning design featured a suspension bridge with a steel, riveted structure and 20 m load-bearing elements resting on masonry pylons lined with granite, designed by Robert Wyerauch and Martin Mayer, a Hamburg-based architect. Construction of the Imperial Bridge (Kaiserbrücke), with boulevards and riverbanks, cost a staggering price of three million German Marks. Although numerous cheaper solutions had been available by then, the city authorities insisted on producing a magnificent structure which would offer a panoramic view of the Tumski and Piaskowa isles. The bridge was commissioned on 10 October 1919. Destroyed during World War II, the pillars of the bridge were reconstructed in the year 1946 according to a design by architect Dobrosław Czajka. In 2005, the car lanes were expanded at the expense of the pavements within the framework of a renovation project.

Photo: Jar Ciurus

Photo: Bartek Barczyk

Water Tower on Groba Street ↑ 037 C

14 Na Grobli Street
Johann Christian Zimmermann
1867–1871

Completed in 1871, this 40 m water tower was the key element of the design created by the English engineer James Moore. His intent was to fulfill the water demands of the city, which, by then, included nearly 200,000 residents. His design was selected in a competition announced by the city authorities in 1861. The overall shape of this 40 m building, erected on a square floor plan and divided into four parts inside, was determined by the city's construction councilman Zimmermann. Initially, the tower contained a single steel riveted water tank. However, further on, in 1902, a second, reinforced concrete tank was added. The total capacity of both tanks was 4,150 m^3. The devices installed at the turn of the nineteenth and twentieth centuries worked until the 1960s, when they were conclusively put out of use. Today, we can marvel at the tower's completely preserved devices, such as steam engines featuring Europe's largest flywheel with a total diameter of 7.5 m. Among other preserved elements are numerous nineteenth-century architectural details, such as, for example, the exquisite, richly decorated spiral staircase. Gradually renovated, the building is still the property of the Municipal Waterworks Company. Due to its unique character, the building has been primarily used by artists, such as the local Ad Spectatores Theatre which has been regularly performing here.

Water Tower on Wiśniowa Alley 038 A

125a Sudecka Street
Karl Klimm
1903–1904

Erected in the southern part of the city, the tower is an intriguing example of Late Eclecticism. The openwork core of the tower was a unique solution, never before applied in any of the European waterworks structures of that age. The building combined Art Nouveau decorations (ornaments, sculptures, copulas) with neo-Gothic forms (the vault above the water tank) and neo-Romanesque expressions (the octagonal part covered with a kiln roof, once containing the water tank). The application of brick supports in the epoch of reinforced concrete also proved the originality of Klimm's design. Initially, the first two storeys were dedicated to residences of the tower's technical staff. This 62 m building equipped with a small view gallery became a tourist attraction at the beginning of the twentieth century. Since 1906, at a small charge, residents and guests were able to discover the panorama of the city. On sunny days they would even catch sight of the distant Karkonosze Mountains. During the siege of Wrocław, the tower served as a viewpoint. The tower has been listed in the register of monuments since 1978. In the 1980s, it would still fulfill an important role in the city's water supply system. At the end of the 1990s, the site was bought by a private investor. The tower was thoroughly renovated under the supervision of Wacław Bieniasz-Nicholson. Currently, the tower houses a restaurant complex.

Photo: Philipp Meuser

District Court and Detention Centre 039 B

1-3 Sądowa/Podwale Street

Karl Ferdinand Busse (1845–1852), Oskar Knorr (1881–1887), Werner Haberland (1930)

In the 1830s, Wrocław started to experience a shortage of prisoner incarceration space. As a result, the location of a new prison was approved in 1839 and a suitable design was created by the architect L. Drewitz. However, due to lengthy procedures, a pertinent agreement was made with the King of Prussia only in 1842. A design by Karl Ferdinand Busse, who specialised in prison development, was selected for execution. As a result, a court-prison complex was erected in a quarter surrounded by the streets of Sądowa, Podwale, Muzealna and Świebodzka. The complex comprised a two-wing masonry court building as well as a prison situated inside the quarter, erected on the Greek cross floor plan. What is noteworthy in terms of the design is the tall corner tower resembling a Gothic castle which serves as the main entrance. The two corner towers housing staircases, elevated avant-corps and horizontal façade divisions create a monumental character. The complex was reconstructed twice. Oskar Knorr extended the court building nearly twofold. In turn, in 1930, Werner Haberland replaced the old wing (from the side of Sądowa Street) with a completely new Modernist building, which ideally completed the monumental character of the entire complex. The site survived World War II and has been fulfilling its primary function ever since.

All photos: Philipp Meuser

University Library
7/9 Karola Szajnochy Street
Richarda Plüddemann
1887–1891

040 B

Construction of the Municipal Savings and Credit Union and the Municipal Library building designed by the city architect Plüddemann was preceded by the reconstruction of a part of the Old Town. The spacious Karlplatz (the current Bohaterów Getta Square) was created with the purpose of serving as the building's front yard. The tight form of the neo-Gothic building was ornamented by a quadrilateral clock tower passing into an octagon. The tower was crowned with a spire copula on a square floor plan. The red masonry façade was enriched by sandstone details. Blackened and soiled, the façade has ceased to impress as it used to in its prime. Due to various functional requirements, the building was to contain, among other things, a vast archive. This did not prevent the designer from creating a beautiful interior décor. The visitor's eye is caught by the representative staircase and the cross vault resting on magnificent pillars. The façade is decorated by a meticulously executed Wrocław coat of arms. The building has been preserved in nearly unchanged condition and currently houses the University Library. Unfortunately, due to a limited budget, the University cannot afford a comprehensive renovation of the building.

Source: iStock (Mariusz Szczygiel)

St. Anthony Church 041 A
26 Jana Kasprowicza Alley
Ludwig Schneider
1900–1901

Built behind the northern bank of River Odra, the St. Anthony of Padua Church in today's Karłowice is part of a sacral complex belonging to the Franciscan Order, which also includes a cloister designed by Joseph Ebers, built between 1895 and 1897. The masonry temple was designed as a three-aisle basilica surrounded by buttresses with a quasi-transept. A flèche capped with a spiky copula was placed above the wide main aisle. The narrow side aisles were covered with cross-ribbed vaults. The interior was divided by inter-aisle pillars. The three-span tube organ choir was also vaulted. In 1903, a large thirty-four-tube organ with a pneumatic tracker action was installed in the church. The original neo-Gothic furnishing was preserved in the interior. Visitors can marvel at the beautiful stained glass elements in the windows of the side aisles and the presbytery. The church survived the war nearly intact. The flèche which was destroyed during the siege of the city was reconstructed in 1979 and the pipe organ was renovated in 2003. Today, the church is the site of numerous concerts.

Source: iStock (Mariusz Szczygiel)

The Clinics

042 C

Chałubińskiego Street et al.
Ludwig von Tiedemann,
Joseph Waldhausen
1887–1909

At the end of the nineteenth century, an idea was put forward to build a complex of clinics and institutes. The author of the first neo-Gothic concept was Ludwig von Tieddemann. Ultimately the construction of a complex featuring a pavilion layout, designed by Joseph Waldhausen, commenced in 1887. The buildings were situated in direct vicinity of the river and green areas. The entire project was based on strict cooperation with physicians, thanks to which one of the most innovative and functional medical facilities of that time was created. The urban complex, which initially comprised school offices and a research hospital, was gradually developed, adding, among other things, a pavilion for patients with tuberculosis. The hospital had the most advanced surgery block in Europe (commissioned in 1897) as well as a chemical-bacteriological laboratory. The complex survived the war in a good condition. Unfortunately, after the war, its layout was condensed in a chaotic manner, i.e. the internal yards were developed, and renovations were carried out without exercising due diligence. It was only in 2010 that the complex was thoroughly renovated. The façades of the buildings were cleaned, the roofs were repaired and the window carpentry was renovated. Today, this magnificent complex is an exquisite monument depicting the progress of medicine.

Photos: Philipp Meuser

Aerial view along the Oder River (2015)

Source: iStock (Mariusz Szczygieł)

Wybrzeże Wyspiańskie Tenement (116)

The Clinics (042)

Stara Odra

Source: iStock (Paweł Szczepański)

The Monopol Hotel 043 B
2 Heleny Modrzejewskiej Street
Brost & Grosser
1892

Erected in 1892 in the place of the former church cemetery, this Art Nouveau hotel building with the adjoining department store soon became one of the showcases of the city. With sixty-nine elegantly furnished rooms, the hotel has always attracted exclusive guests. The department store was destroyed during the war and then reconstructed in 1961, whereas the hotel was preserved in its entirety. After the war, the Monopol and the café situated in the reconstructed department store became the elegant meeting spots for the local elite. Some of the most prominent guests to visit the hotel were Marlene Dietrich, Mikhail Sholokhov and Pablo Pocasso, who attended the World Intellectual Congress of 1948. In 1958, Jan Kiepura sang from the very balcony which was built in 1937 for Hitler himself. The building would often serve as a film location. It was here that Andrzej Wajda filmed several of his cult shots to *Ash and Diamond*. In 1984, the building was listed in the Wrocław monument register. In the 1990s, the Monopol café closed and its original commercial function was restored. In turn, in 2007 the hotel was bought by a private investor, who carried

Photo: Philipp Meuser

Photo: Philipp Meuser

out its general renovation and extension, recreating, among other things, the tower crowning the corner of the building from the side of Świdnicka Street. Reconstruction works were supervised by the architect Marcin Janowski. Nowadays, the building houses a luxury five-star hotel.

The Palace 044 B
34 Kościuszki Street
Karl Heidenreich
1889–1890

This impressive three-wing palace of Hans Ulrich von Schaffgotsch, which was designed by Karl Heidenreich, was erected on the site of the former villa built upon a square floor plan. This two-storey, Renaissance edifice has two perpendicular wings covered with a steep gable roof. The masonry façade is ornamented with sandstone details. The body is linked to the western wing with a spectacular four-storey tower crowned with a copula. One of the most characteristic elements of the building are the avant-corps with bay windows, typical for Victorian architecture. In 1915, the palace was taken over by the evangelical commune, and some of the rooms were adapted for offices. After the war, the palace served as a residential estate. In 1957, by decision of the Communist authorities, the building was passed over to the Association of Polish Students, thanks to which it served as an art and entertainment centre. Jan Grotowski would stage his first performances here; in addition, the legendary Kalambur Theatre created by Bogusław Litwiniec operated here. For years, the palace, or rather its interiors, housed the Academic Culture Centre – the Little Palace, hence the popular name of this building. In the year 2012, the Student Association sold the building to a private investor.

All photos: Philipp Meuser

National Museum ←↓

045 B

5 Powstańców Warszawy Street
Karl Friedrich Endell
1883–1886

The construction of this magnificent residence of the Silesian Province Management, designed by the Berlin architect Karl Friedrich Endell, commenced in 1883. Situated by the river, the building was to symbolise the power of a united Germany. Erected in the Dutch neo-Renaissance style, the building referred to sixteenth-century German palatial complexes. Its masonry façade was ornamented with sandstone elements, whereas the northern corners of the edifice were crowned with impressive copulas. The building survived World War II nearly intact; thereby, when the National Museum was established on 1 January 1947, this representative edifice was selected as its residence. In 1948, one of the first Polish Painting Galleries was opened in the building. Its collection was enriched by a group of works donated to the institution in 1946 by Soviet-Ukrainian institutions from Lviv and Kyiv.

Supraregional Agricultural Congress Centre ↑

046 A

87/89 Pawłowicka Street
August Orth
1891–1895

In 1886, the son of a wealthy family of publishers and printers – Heinrich Horn – purchased the former Pawłowice grange situated at the southern edge of the Zakrzowski Forest. After dismantling the old development, he created a stunning palace complex designed by August Orth. Extended between 1905 and 1910, this French neo-Renaissance residence comprised a three-wing palace erected on a rectangular floor plan, comprising the southern tower wing, and a link accentuated with a large tower at the centre. The masonry façade of the palace was accentuated with a central avant-corps. The new owners reconstructed the spacious park as well. At the beginning of the twentieth century, they built a monopteros and a fountain within the park. The building, which survived the war in ideal condition, was acquired by the University of Wrocław in 1945. Eight years later, the palace was purchased by the Academy of Natural Sciences which reconstructed its interiors for the purposes of an agricultural test centre. In 1976, following a fire the roof and attic were reconstructed. In 2005, the historical complex was thoroughly renovated, and thanks to the efforts of the Academy and EU funds a congress centre was opened there.

Puppet Theatre 047 B

4 Teatralny Square
Paul Kieschke, Richard Bielenberg
1892–1894

The neo-Baroque residence of the Wrocław Puppet Theatre was built upon the site of the Classicist Brotherhood of the Rooster club residence designed by Carl Gotthard Langhans, serving as the office of the merchants' guild since 1880, referred to as the *Zwinger*. The *Zwinger* was demolished in 1892 due to existing plans to demarcate Teatralny Square. The design was selected in an open competition and outlined the construction of an edifice reflecting the architecture of seventeenth-century French palaces. The edifice would be built on the floor plan of a rectangle extended on the North-South axis, with a characteristic attic level. The main entrance with a portico and a vestibule was placed in the side frontage. An extensive terrace connected the eastern side of the building with a promenade running along the city moat. In 1937, the neo-Baroque interiors of the building were reconstructed to reflect the monumental Third Reich style. After the war, the ideally preserved complex became the residence of the Polish-Soviet Friendship Association, and since 1965 the Chochlik State Puppet Theatre. In 1999, the building was entirely operated by the Wrocław Puppet Theatre. The interiors of the building were reconstructed and in 2005, the façade of the building was restored. A year later, a fountain designed by Paweł Pawlak was built in front of the main entrance of the building and in 2010 the park adjoining the palace was fully restored.

NOT Building 048 B
74 Piłsudskiego Street
Eduard Blummer,
Christian Behrens, Ernst Seger
(façade: 1893–1895)

In the year 1893, the Silesian Province Management purchased a plot on the then Ogrodowa Street (former Gardenstrasse) to build a new office for the Silesian State Assembly. This task was entrusted to the state construction inspector Blumner. Construction works commenced in 1893 and were completed in June 1895. The design is modelled on similar developments from Hanover, Dresden and other German cities and reflected the layout of a representative French palace. The end result comprised a reverse T-shape edifice. The wider façade with small side wings, designed by Christian Behrens and Ernst Seger (the winners of the competition), was situated on Piłsudskiego Street. Inside, apart from the assembly room, visitors will find a beautiful yard covered with a glazed roof. In 1938, the assembly room was reconstructed to provide space for the Atom cinema house. Following the war, the building was taken over by the Wrocław division of the Supreme Technical Organisation (Naczelna Organizacja Techniczna – NOT). In 1977, the building was entered to the register of monuments. Ever since the 1990s, the building has fulfilled various functions, although it has remained the residence of the Wrocław Council of Scientific – Technical Association Federation. Recent years have been marked by numerous efforts to restore the edifice to its original splendour.

All photos: Philipp Meuser

Wrocław SPA Centre
10/12 Teatralna Street
Wilhelm Werdelmann (1897)
Herbert Eras (extension: 1925–1927)

049 B

In 1895, the company Breslauer Hallenschwimmbad AG announced a competition for a public lavatory design. The winning design was by Wilhelm Werdelman, an architect originating from Leipzig, and proposed the construction of a complex of masonry buildings housing various functions, such as a swimming pool etc. The swimming pool halls feature strong reinforced concrete structures. Commissioned in the year 1897, the building proved so popular among the residents of Wrocław that it had to be extended twice. The final shape of the complex was affected by the extension initiated in 1925, when, according to Herbert Eras' design, the swimming pool building was elevated by two storeys. The lavatory survived the war without incurring any significant damage and in the summer of 1945 it was reopened to the public. From 1960 to 1962, the complex underwent upgrading works which unfortunately destroyed a significant part of the original furnishing and décor. In 1977, the complex was listed in the register of monuments.

Tenements on Miernicza Street

050 B

Miernicza Street
1866–1899

Formerly known as Lützowstraße, Miernicza Street was marked out in 1866 on a plot belonging to the Cassirer&Söhne trading company in such a manner that it linked the two streets Traugutta and Komuny Paryskiej. Until the end of the nineteenth century, the street located in the Przedmieście Oławskie district was densely developed with rent tenements inhabited primarily by the workers of nearby factories. The initial name of the street referred to Baron Ludwik von Lützow, the commanding officer of the voluntary regiment taking part in the war against Napoleon. Due to its working-class milieu, the street had a bad repute. After the war, it was incorporated into the so-called *Bermuda triangle,* an area one should never stray to. The unique character of the street is proven by the fact that the pre-war development has survived until the present day nearly intact. It thus became an ideal location for filmmakers. Miernicza Street provided the setting for Agnieszka Holland's *A Lonely Woman* and the Oscar-winning *Karakter* by Mike van Diem.

All photos: Philipp Meuser

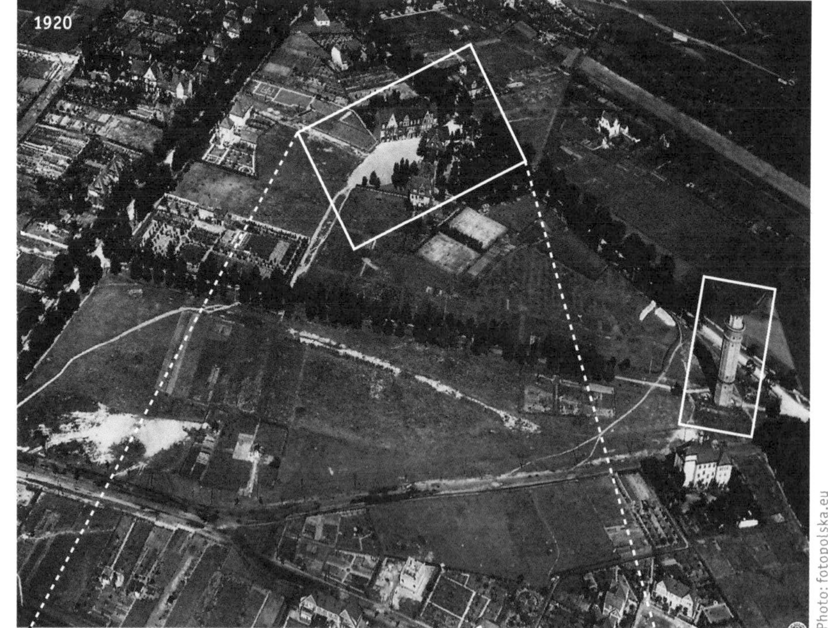

Photo: fotopolska.eu

Photo: fotopolska.eu

Photo: Philipp Meuser

Photo: Philipp Meuser

Karłowice Garden City 051 A
Piłsudskiego Square
Paul Schmitthenner
1911–1913, 1914–1915, 1927

At the turn of the seventeenth and eighteenth centuries, the abbot of the St. Vincent Cloister in Ołbin, Carl Keller, founded a village entitled Carlowitz. Until the beginning of the nineteenth century, inhabited primarily by a Polish population, it was owned by the cloister and was later sold to a private owner. In 1898, the cloister and the Ursuline high school were completed; the neo-Gothic St. Anthony Church and the Franciscan cloister were commissioned in 1901. In turn, 1911 marked the beginning of the construction of a complex designed by Paul Schmitthenner at the request of the company Eigenheim Baugesellschaft für Deutschland. Its urban design referred to the increasingly popular idea of a city garden, expressed by Ebenezer Howard in *Garden Cities of Tomorrow*. It was only in 1913 that Gartenstadt Karlowitz comprised thirty-three houses. In 1914, the construction of a trapezoid complex intended for commercial and cultural purposes (Am Markt) commenced. In 1915, the company Lolat Eisbeton Breslau AG built an Early Modernist reinforced concrete water tower of 45 m in Karłowice. A year before the city was incorporated in Breslau, the market square underwent a second development stage in which a monument commemorating German soldiers fallen in World War I was erected. After 1945, the monument was dismantled. In 1935 the Higher Seminary was completed (currently the Faculty of Biotechnology at the University of Wrocław); the building was designed by Anton Mokroß. The central square in Karłowice was named after Józef Piłsudski.

Kamieniecka Street and Tarnogaj Estate

052 A

Kamieniecka Street
Paul Schreiber, Hans Thomas
1919–1920, 1928–1931, 1937

In the year 1904, the Tarnogaj municipality (German: Dürrgoy) was incorporated into Wrocław. A year later, a modern but historic gas company building designed by Matthias Wirtz was opened. He also developed a design for a worker colony aimed at the employees of the building. Its urban concept made reference to the ideas of the renowned Viennese architect and urban planner, Camillo Sitte. Unfortunately, reflecting the idea of a *Landhaus*, the design inspired by a Berlin *Wohnhof*-type development was not completed. In 1919, Paul Schreiber created a design for a worker settlement encompassing the areas enclosed by the streets Tarnogajska, Morwowa, Ziębicka and Księdza Czesława Klimasa. The design also included the construction of one-storey single-family houses with tall roofs decorated with dormers on the side facing the street and with shared utility wings from the side of the gardens. A total of 140 houses in two rows were built on the two streets Kamieniecka and Ziębicka. In 1920, according to Schreiber's design, seven two-storey multi-family houses were built upon Gazowa Street. Between 1928 and 1931, a series of three-storey multi-family houses with tall roofs were built on Tarnogórska Street, all according to a design by Wilhelm Hogreve. The last stage of the works was the development of Złotostocka Street with four rows of four-storey masonry houses with flat roofs, designed by Hans Thomas. The development on Kamieniecka Street has been the sole one to survive fully intact.

All photos: Philipp Meuser

Source: iStock (Velishchuk)

St. Augustine Parish 053 A

90 Sudecka Street

Alfred Böttcher, Richard Gaze

1909

An evangelical temple presenting an eclectic composition of Art Nouveau, Romanesque – and even Byzantine elements (characteristic of Late Historicism) – was built in 1909. The temple was erected on a Greek cross floor plan with nine towers. The transept is enclosed by a semi-circular apse surrounded by a ring of enfilade chapels and sacristies. A massive nine-storey tower of 78 m, covered with a steep pyramid copula roofed with copper plates, ascends from the junction of the transept and the aisles. The lower and the highest storeys of the tower are surrounded by terraces, crowned with four towers in the corners which are also covered with pyramidal copulas. This evangelical temple, which was nearly destroyed in half during the war, was purchased by the Catholic Church in 1948. Its reconstruction was completed in the autumn of 1949. The interior of the church impresses with its altar crucifix made of canary marble (according to a design by R. Schipke), contemporary stained glass elements executed according to a design by J. Stańda which present St. Francis of Assisi and Mary in the Glory of Space, as well as the historical wall pulpit designed by Theodor von Gosen, made of black marble. The church boasts a forty-eight-tube organ featuring an electrical and pneumatic tracker action, created by the Wrocław organ master Józef Cynar.

Photo: Philipp Meuser

St. Charles Boromeo Church

054 A

58 Krucza Street
Ludwig Schneider, Józef Maas
1910–1913

The year 1913 marked the completion of a temple designed by Ludwig Schneider and Józef Maas, situated in a quarter enclosed by the streets Gajowicka, Krucza and Grochowa. The church was erected on the site of the former chapel. The neo-Romanesque form of the church refers to the architecture of the Rhineland. The three-aisle structure of the building was made of crude stone and includes a quadrilateral tower on the western side. The interior is covered by a cross-ribbed vault resting on eight pillars. The building is decorated with four corner towers. During the siege of the city that took place in the year 1945, the church was transformed into a stronghold which resulted in its extensive damage during one of the bombarding raids. In the aftermath of the war, various ideas for developing the temple were proposed. One of these, for example, outlined the creation of a garrison church. Ultimately the first partial reconstruction of the building started in 1947 and took four years. In 1985, the building was listed in the Wrocław register of monuments. The same year, the second thorough renovation of the temple commenced, which ended in 1987. The church pipe organ also underwent a general renovation in the year 2008. Recent years have been marked by the restoration of the façade.

Photo: Philipp Meuser

Sułkowice Mill
35 Poprzeczna Alley
1890

055 A

This monumental neo-Gothic masonry building was erected in 1890 at the request of the company Schlesische Mühlenwerke A.G. Its asymmetrical extended form with a varying number of storeys is covered with a flat roof, including a series of smaller buildings (fulfilling, among other things, various administrative functions) to create a unique industrial complex. Its south-western corner is crowned with a historic tower, and its façades are ornamented with sandstone elements. In 1925, a five-storey granary with a three-storey apex, covered with a gable roof connected with the main building via a footbridge was erected to the south of the complex. After the war, the complex was modernised twice. At the end of the 1990s, production was gradually terminated. Several proposals for developing the complex were raised at the beginning of the twenty-first century. A market was opened there in 2008. In 2010, the building was listed in the register of monuments which did not prevent the new owner of the complex, the company domExpo (which planned to renovate and transform it into an exhibition centre) demolishing the 1925 granary in 2013. The investor announced that the complex designed by AGK Architekci would be opened soon.

Photo: Philipp Meuser

Photo: Philipp Meuser

Railway Embankment on Bogusławskiego Street

056 B

Bogusławskiego Street
1905

Construction of this 600 m long overpass comprising six viaducts and sixty-seven masonry vaults was completed in 1905. The structure was built to improve the traffic throughput and facilitate the development of the city towards the south. Elevating the Poznań-Wrocław railway line enabled the elimination of one-level junctions of railway tracks and roads. The overpass survived the siege of the city in very good condition, although German forces adapted part of the spans for the purpose of shelters. The overpass is a unique example of the spontaneous revitalisation of part of the urban space, as well as of the symbiosis of industrial architecture with the fabric of the contemporary city. Although a number of restaurants and bars functioned here prior to the war, after 1945 the spans were primarily used as both warehouses and garages. At the end of the 1990s, the overpass attracted residents once more. The first bars and stores were thus created. In recent years, the overpass has been gradually renovated. Due to the close proximity of various cultural institutions, such as, for example, the Polish Theatre or the Kapitol Theatre, this location has become an increasingly popular social hub.

Photo: Bartek Barczyk

Source: iStock (Mariusz Szczygiel)

Faculty of Architecture of the University of Technology ↑

057 A

53/55 Prusa Street

Karl Klimm, Richard Plüddemann

1904

Erected at the turn of the nineteenth and twentieth centuries, this building complex is one of the most outstanding examples of the Wrocław Art Nouveau trend. The complex comprises the School of Construction Craftsmanship building, the Higher School of Machine Construction building and the Johann Heinrich Pestalozzi Folk School Complex building. The complex was designed by Richard Plüddemann, the city architect, and the execution of the design was entrusted to Karl Klimm. In turn, Gustav Hasse was in charge of the construction works. The buildings were built of brick and stone, and the façade was covered with lime plaster bearing a striped structure. Their tall roofs were covered with glazed tiles, glass tiles and glass. What is noteworthy about the complex is the magnificent clock tower connecting the mutually shifted wings of the edifice, including the entrance leading to both schools, as well as the richly ornamented auditorium situated on the last floor of the vocational school under the exposed truss roof structure. Inside the tower is a preserved ceiling base frieze covered with polychromies, created by Hans Rumsch. The machine laboratory building was severely damaged at the end of World War II, whereas the remaining part of the complex survived in good condition. After the war, the building was taken over by the Faculty of Botany of the University of Wrocław. Between 1968 and 1970, the Faculty of Architecture of the Wrocław University of Technology moved here.

Institute of Pedagogy and Institute of Psychology of the University of Wrocław ↗→

058 A

1 J. Wł. Dawida Street

Karl Klimm, Richard Plüddemann, Julius Nathansohn

1903

Erected between 1901 and 1903, this edifice designed by Klimm, Plüddemann and Nathansohn (extended in 1913) was created to serve as a residence for the St. Elizabeth Gymnasium operating in Wrocław until the end of the thirteenth century. Built on an L-shaped floor plan, the building contained spacious lecture halls situated from the side of the large afforested yard (east and south), linked with a long corridor running from the west. Such a layout provided optimal lighting in the building and protected the interiors against the noise of the street. A large wooden-structure auditorium ornamented with Art Nouveau

Photo: Philipp Meuser

stained glass elements, paintings and sculptures was situated on the second floor. Unfortunately, these furnishing elements have not been preserved today. The form of the building is accentuated by decorative apexes and towers, avant-corps and a dynamic roof layout. Windows of varying size add another level of dynamism to the building. Apart from the main building, the complex also houses a gym, a principal's villa and a yard. The overall construction costs exceeded half a million German Marks. The complex survived World War II without incurring any major damage. Today, the building houses the Institute of Pedagogy and the Institute of Psychology of the University of Wrocław.

Photo: Philipp Meuser

Feniks Department Store **059 B**
31-32 Rynek/75 Szewska Street
Georg Schneider
1904

Erected in 1904 on the site of the demolished Pod Złotym Dzbanem tenement, the Barasch Brothers' Department Store building designed by Georg Schneider was deservedly named the Temple of Commerce. This Art Nouveau building of 8,000 m² impressed not only with its innovative solutions, such as elevators, central steam heating and electrical lighting, but also with the opulence of marble, bronze and glass interior elements built according to plans by Julius Koblinsky. Visitors would marvel at the sandstone, iron and bronze façade with enormous glass display windows. The corner tower of the building was crowned by an illuminated globe, with a total diameter of 6.5 m, resting on four sphinxes. Unfortunately, the globe was destroyed at the end of the 1920s by a bolt of lightning and was never reconstructed again. Between the years 1928 and 1930, the Simon&Halfpaap architectural company reconstructed the building. As a result, the internal yard covered with a glass roof was demolished and the glazed façade replaced by a simple four-axis façade. All Art Nouveau ornaments were also removed. In 1938, fearing persecution, the Barasch brothers sold the building and left the country. After the war, the building was handed over to the Społem Co-op and, between 1961 and 1965, was thoroughly modernised. Since 1965, the building has housed the Feniks department store.

»With Marcin Szczelina as a guide, the beauty of this place becomes clear and evident, even if its glories are so much in the past. But at night, it comes alive in other ways… «

Aaron Betsky

Wrocław, old city centre

Source: iStock (mrybsk)

Source: iStock (kocur)

Photo: Thomas Michael Krüger

How to Use this Architectural Guide

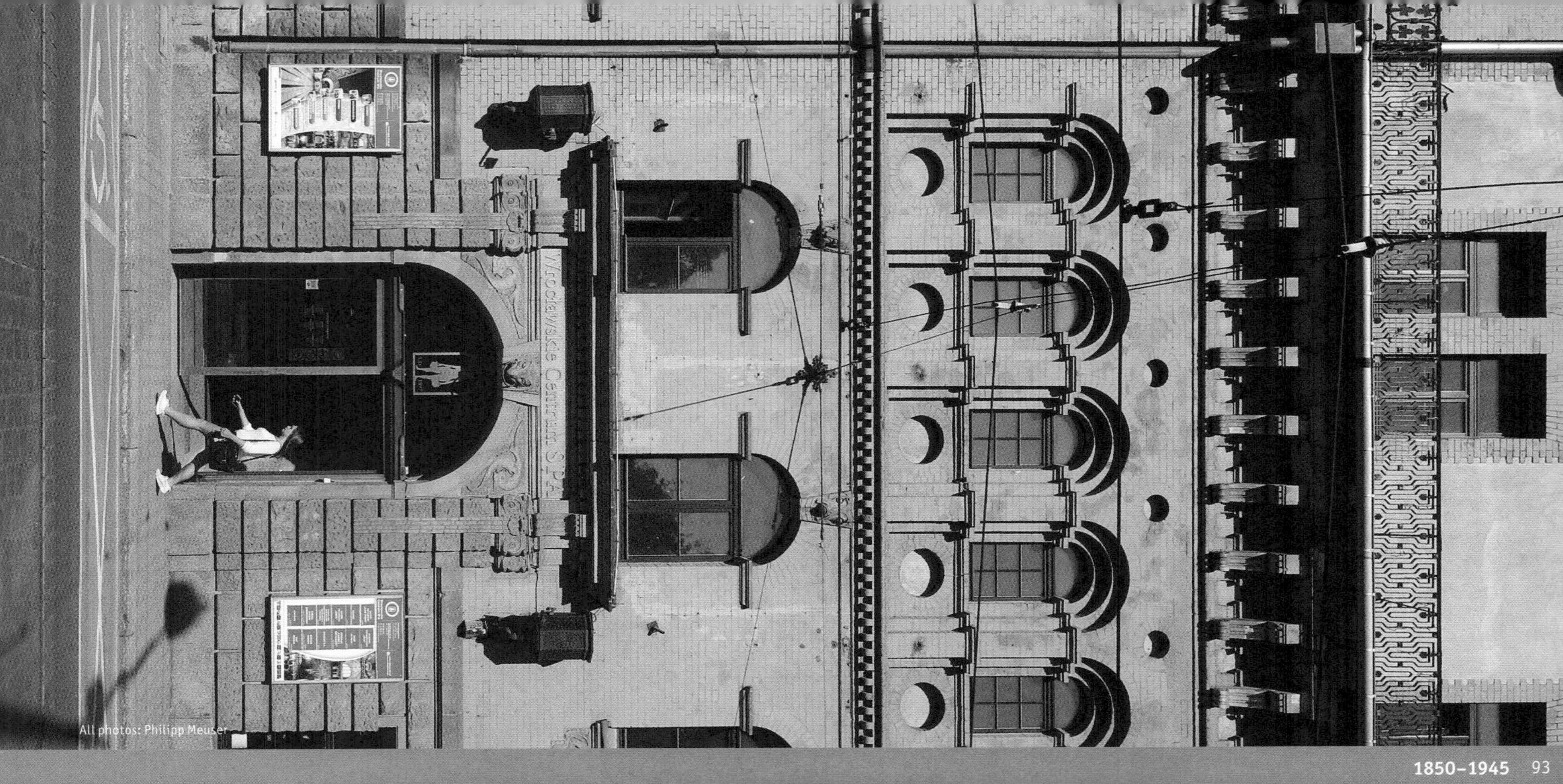

All photos: Philipp Meuser

WZZ Herbapol Offices (Former Victoria Department Store) **060** **B**

65/68 Św. Mikołaja St./
26/27 Rzeźnicza Street
Georg Harter
1900

Built in 1900 in the place of five tenements, the Victoria Department Store building (Victoriahaus), designed by the architect and investor Georg Harter, has housed one of the first cinemas in the city since 1906. The four-storey corner building with a modern reinforced concrete frame structure, an internal yard covered with a gable roof and a sandstone façade ornamented with plant decoration housed the owner's flat featuring an impressive grated terrace on the highest floor. Resting on a pillar, the corner bay crowned with a tower was decorated with a statue of Victoria with putto. The building continues to impress with its wooden entrance gates decorated with wrought iron plant motifs, as well as coats of arms presenting the symbols of liberated arts, commerce, industry and transport situated above the second-storey window arches. Since 1942, the building has also housed the VIATIK-ZIGARETTENFABRIK cigarette factory. After the war, the building was sold to the Herbapol Herbal Company in 1956.

All photos: Philipp Meuser

32/33

All photos: Philipp Meuser

Schlesinger & Grünbaum Department Store ← 061 B

32/33 Rzeźnicka Street
Leo Schlesinger
1899–1901

In 1899, the company Schlesinger and Grünbaum, the manufacturer and trader ofmen'sandchildren'sfashion, purchased two plots on Rzeźnicka Street, the original location of a building housing the Karl Linke steam engine construction workshop and the Pod Trzema Górami drive-in. The building designed by Schlesinger is an example of a frame reinforced concrete structure, in which each storey is supported by slim cantilevers only, allowing for a random and unobstructed arrangement of internal space. The Art Nouveau façade of this four-storey building has eight richly ornamented structural pillars which, at the level of the fourth floor, connect to form nearly complete arches. From the street level, the space between the pillars is filled with giant windows. The design of the building refers to the Tiedmann department store in Berlin. In the 1930s, the building was acquired by the Muelle&Co confectionery company. After the war, the building became the residence of the Intermoda Clothing Industry Company. Since its renovation in 1991, an Intermoda company store has been operating on both the ground and first floors.

Pokoyhof Arcade ↑ 062 B

2/4 Świętego Antoniego Street
Alexis Langer (1853)
Karl Heintz (1910)
Renovation: 2011

This building complex located between the streets Włodkowica and Świętego Antoniego has been referred to as Pokyhof since the seventeenth century, probably owing to the name of the first owner of the drive-in for the Jews visiting the city for commercial purposes: Bartłomiej Pokquaiesa. The name Buquoihof is first encountered in historical materials dating back to 1624 The buildings were completely destroyed by a major explosion in the gunpowder room in 1749. The arcade was gradually created to ultimately attain its final shape. First, a neo-Gothic building designed by Alexis Langer, a German architect, was erected in 1853 to serve a hotel function. In 1910 a modern shopping arcade, designed by Karl Heintze, was built at the request of the Pokyhof Construction Society on Świętego Antoniego Street. The arcade is an example of an Early Modernist reinforced concrete structure featuring a simple façade with wide windows. After the war, the building, as well as the entire neighbourhood, fell into demise. In 2007, a general renovation of the Pokyhof was initiated. The façade was ornamented with a glass green mosaic with golden frames, imported from Venice.

Bruno Löffelholz Tenement
5 Bolesława Prusa Street
Wilhelm Heller
1902

063 A

Since the urban design plans created in the 1870s for the right Odra River bank, a period of dynamic development within this part of the city has commenced. In 1902, a unique tenement designed by Wilhelm Heller was built on Prusa Street for the architect Bruno Löffelholz. This five-storey edifice with an attic, an asymmetric façade, three two-storey bays and two staircases situated at the external ends of the building was built on a broad arch floor plan. The façade is crowned with a dominating cornice vaulted to the outside, covered with a beautiful polychromy depicting the horizon and embracing a plant motif. The internal layout of the building is adapted to the floor plan; therefore the front rooms are trapezoidal. Two entrance portals enclosed with a complete arch ornamented with stuccowork featuring plant motifs lead to the interior of the building. The building was thoroughly renovated in 2006. Since then, the tenement has been one of the most impressive Art Nouveau villas in the city.

Photo: Philipp Meuser

Hieronimus 1 (The Glass House) 064 B

34 Świdnicka Street/
8 Teatralny Square

Paul and Richard Ehrlich (1911), Anita Luniak, Teresa Mromlińska (reconstruction: 2013)

In the year 1910, the Ehrlich brothers built an elegant tenement at the request of a wealthy merchant and philanthropist on the corner of Świdnicka Street and Teatralny Square. This six-storey Early Modernist building with a reinforced concrete frame structure, as well as a rounded corner enclosing a roofed yard, refers to the Chicago School of Architecture. The building housed the St. Hieronimus department store. The façade was covered with richly ornamented pink sandstone lining. After the war, the interiors of the building were reconstructed. The ground floor retained its commercial function. Its higher floors, however, were devoted to a dormitory of the University of Wrocław, also referred to as the Glass House, which was later transformed into a language school and the Faculty of Social Sciences of the University of Wrocław. The building is currently owned by a private investor. In 2014, a thorough renovation of the building was carried out according to a design by Grupa 33_03 which proposed, among other things, the recreation of the primary façades and glazing elements, the reconstruction of the functional layout and the creation and design of attic space.

Renoma

065 B

40 Świdnicka Street
Hermann Dernburg (1930), Maćków Pracownia Projektowa (extension: 2005-2009)

The Wertheim Department Store – the largest department store in Wrocław – was officially opened on 2 April 1930. The author of the design of this Modernist edifice, who won the competition announced in 1927, was Hermann Dernburg. A seven-storey building with two internal yards covered with a glass roof at the level of the first floor, rounded corners and large display windows on the ground floor, was then erected. The last storeys of the building are gradually withdrawn into the centre. The front façade is glazed with ceramics and crossed with strips of windows encircling the building. The entire body is completed by ornaments created by the sculptors Ulrich Nitschke and Hans Klakow. Dernburg's design initially proposed the further extension of the building on Czysty Square (Salvatorplatz); however, these plans were thwarted by the Great Depression. In 1937, the department store belonging to the Wertheim family was acquired by the AWAG company established by the Nazis (Allgemeine Warenhaus Gesellschaft). In March 1945, the building was bombarded, but then reopened in 1948 for the *Recovered Territory Exhibition*. Successive floors were renovated and commissioned throughout the following years, until 1985. In 1977, the building was listed in the monument register. A competition for the name of the building was carried out in the *Słowo Polskie* magazine. Renoma was the winning name. At the end of the 1990s, the building was taken over by a private owner, who in 2005 launched an extension and general renovation of the building, supervised by the Maćków design office, which lasted four years.

All photos: Philipp Meuser

065 B

Kameleon Department Store **066 B**

6/7 Szewska St./7 Oławska St.
Erich Mendelsohn
1928

The department store was erected on the corner of the streets Szewska and Oławska, according to a design by Erich Mendelsohn, a renowned architect. The six-storey building impresses with its corner bay connecting two different façades. The representative façade from the side of Szewska Street consists of horizontal lines of glass display windows, divided by protruding cornices. The interiors of the building completed at the request of Rudolf Petersdorff's company were designed by architect and artist Heinrich Tischner. Apart from stores, the building also housed a warehouse, offices and Petersdorf production halls. In 1939, as a result of the persecution of the Jewish community, the department store was handed over to the Dyckhoff textile company, which used the building as its own department store until 1945. The building was damaged at the end of World War II. In the 1960s, the building underwent renovation and was then listed in the register of monuments in 1962. In 2007, the building was renovated and reconstructed according to a design by KMA Kabarowski Misiura Architekci. Within the course of reconstruction, a part of the Modernist character of the interiors was lost.

Photo: Thomas Michael Krüger

Photo: Philipp Meuser

Poelzig Office and Commercial Building

067 B

38/40 Ofiar Oświęcimskich St.
Hans Poelzig
1913

Situated on the corner of the streets Ofiar Oświęcimskich and Laciarka, this magnificent building designed by the renowned Modernist architect, lecturer and director of the National Academy of Arts and Crafts in Wrocław, Hans Poelzig, was erected at the request of Junkernstraße-Baugesellschaft m.b.H. This innovative reinforced concrete structure featuring open interiors, devoid of any decorations or functionalist façades, became an icon of local architecture. The modest façade, including large display windows on the ground floor, featured large, triple windows on the higher levels and a raw concrete structure devoid of any decorative elements – with the exception of the openwork balustrade of the shallow terrace enclosing the fifth retracted storey. It was Poelzig who first established this horizontal division of the façade and with such success. This feature dominated the architecture of public buildings in Wrocław in the 1920s. The building housed stores, a cinema house, offices and the city merchant school for boys and girls. Following World War II, the last floor was added and the roof was reconstructed.

Photo: Thomas Michael Krüger

Photo: Philipp Meuser

Quantum Oławska Office Building ↑

068 B

10-11 Oławska Street
Sepp Kaiser
1931

The C&A Department Store designed by artist and architect Sepp Kaisner was built in Wrocław in 1931 at the request of the Brenninkmeijer brothers. The building was erected on the site of the demolished Hotel Weisser Adler (White Eagle). The Modernist five-storey corner edifice featuring a reinforced concrete pile-nogging structure was built with a rectangular floor plan on the ground floor and with an L-shaped plan on the upper storeys. The ground floor had a uniformly glazed façade. The façade on the upper floors was formed out of staggered horizontal strips of windows and travertine-lined walls. This raw form, nearly devoid of decorations, featured a corner connection between the eastern and northern façades resembling the bay structure found in the Kameleon. Here, the corner was a rounded overhang crowned with a copper roof. The last storey from the side of Łaciarska Street was retracted. The building's modern form was complemented by neon lights. In 1937, similar to other local department stores, the building was acquired by Allgemeine Warenhaus Gesellschaft GmbH, or AWAG. After the war, the building housed, among other things, the Wrocław Graphic Studio. The building, which is currently privately owned, underwent a thorough renovation in the year 2012.

Market Hall ↗→

069 B

17 Piaskowa Street
Richard Plüddemann, Friedrich Friese, Heinrich Küster
1906–1908

At the end of the nineteenth century, a plan to erect four modern market halls was put forward to replace the open markets in the city. Ultimately, only two of these were completed, both of which were designed by the construction adviser Richard Plüddemanna, Friedricha Friese and engineer Heinrich Küster. The market hall located on 16 Piaskowa Street is the sole market hall to still exist. Displaying simplified neo-Gothic and Art Nouveau elements from the outside, the building

Photo: Thomas Michael Krüger

reveals an innovative reinforced concrete structure from the inside. The main room rests on six parabolic arches with a total span of 19 m. Hall No. 1 was crowned with a corner clock tower resembling a defence tower, referring to medieval city fortifications. The entrance to the hall is ornamented by Art Nouveau elements, and the Wrocław coat of arms has been placed at the western and eastern tips of the building. The western tower is decorated by the bas-relief of Carl Ulbrich. The building survived the war in nearly ideal condition; therefore it was reopened to the public almost immediately after the end of the war. Between the years 1980 and 1982, the building underwent a general renovation during which the original chessboard and the majority of the stands were removed.

Photo: Thomas Michael Krüger

TKANINY
ZEGARMISTRZ
LOTTO
5 in 1!

Photo: Philipp Meuser

Source: iStock (Santiago Rodriguez Fonto)

Centennial Hall ↑↓

1 Wystawowa Street

Max Berg

1911–1913

070 C

The Centennial Hall, erected between 1911 and 1913 for the Centennial Exhibition (according to a design by architect and engineer Max Berg) is, without any doubt, a unique site. In 2006, Berg's work was entered to the UNESCO World Heritage List. A need to create a recreational exhibition centre – which would meet the expectations and aspirations of the developing city – was formulated in the nineteenth century. Ultimately a visionary though controversial, Berg's design won during an architectural competition for the development of the Exhibition Area, organised by the city authorities. The first works commenced in May 1911 and in December 1912 the contractor, Dyckerhoff & Widmann, commissioned the raw building. Completed in 1913, the Centennial Hall featured the world's largest roofing. The round floor plan

Photo: Thomas Michael Krüger

of the hall, based symmetrically on the Greek cross with its arms terminating with small outbound halls, has an oval two-storey entry hall. The building survived World War II in perfect condition. The World Intellectual Congress to Protect the Country took place in the Centennial Hall in 1948 and was attended by such personalities as Pablo Picasso, Bertolt Brecht and Irene Juliot-Curie. In 1962, the building was entered to the register of monuments. Since then, the building has been recorded on the UNESCO World Heritage List and has undergone a series of renovations.

The Pavilion of Four Copulas ↓ 071 C

38/40 Ofiar Oświęcimskich St.
Hans Poelzig
1913

Erected between 1912 and 1913 as an element of the Centennial Hall building complex, this Modernist pavilion designed by Hans Poelzig comprised two parts – an enfilade series of rooms divided by copulas and an enormous yard. The northern and the southern copulas, built in the shape of ellipses, are larger than the western and eastern ones, erected with a circular floor plan. A sculpture of Athena by Professor Robert Bednorz was placed in the interior roofed garden. The interiors of the building, particularly the rooms, were constructed in such a manner so as to facilitate both the creation of thematic and chronological exhibitions. The investment was executed by Schlesische Beton Baugesellschaft. Following World War II, the building was used by the Wrocław Feature Film Production Company. In 2006, the Pavilion of Four Copular was recognised as a monument of history, and – together with the Centennial Hall – was listed on the UNESCO World Heritage List. In 2009, the building was acquired by the National Museum. In 2013, the building underwent a thorough renovation co-financed by European Union funds. Completed in 2015, the works aimed at adapting the pavilion to the purposes of exhibiting Polish contemporary art. Unfortunately, the effect of the works conducted by Budimex proved highly controversial. In the opinion of specialists, the building lost a part of its historical value as a result of the renovation work.

Source: iStock (Mariusz Szczygiel)

070 C

Photo: Jean Molitor

Source: iStock (Mariusz Szczygiel)

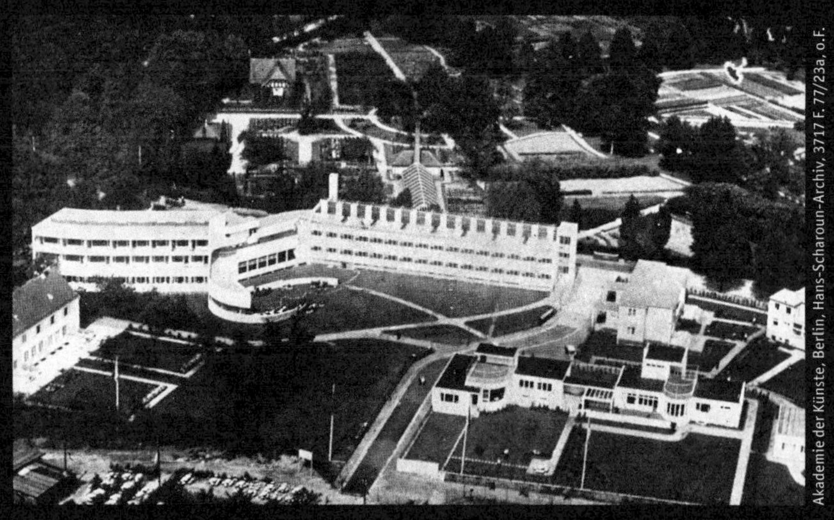
Akademie der Künste, Berlin, Hans-Scharoun-Archiv, 3717 F. 77/23a, o.F.

WuWA

072 C

The streets Tramwajowa, Edwarda Dembowskiego, Mikołaja Kopernika et al.
1929

In the year 1929, the Silesian committee of the Deutsche Werkbund organised the WuWA (German: *Wohnungs- und Werkraum-ausstellung*) residential exhibition in Dąbie, a district of Wrocław, near the Szczytnicki Park. The art directors of the exhibition were Heinrich Lauterbach and Adolf Rading. The exhibition presented thirty-two residential and utility buildings, including both single-family and multi-family houses as well as a model kindergarten. The interiors of the buildings were designed by Anna Rading and Josef Vinecky. One of the most interesting projects included Model House No. 1 on Tramwajowa Street, designed by Paul Heim and Albert Kempter, which is referred to as the multi-family gallery house (*Laubenganghaus*) with kitchens on the western side and residential rooms on the eastern side. Model House No. 2, referred to as the high-rise, was similarly built upon Tramwajowa Street. Initially, Rading's design proposed the construction of two symmetrical ten-storey high-rises with a frame structure, allowing for a random interior design connected by corridors on each floor. Ultimately, the building was reduced to four floors. After the war, several of the buildings were handed over to private users, some of whom modified the buildings according to their own preferences. Scharoun's and Rading's projects still serve as a hotel and a dormitory.

Model (1927)

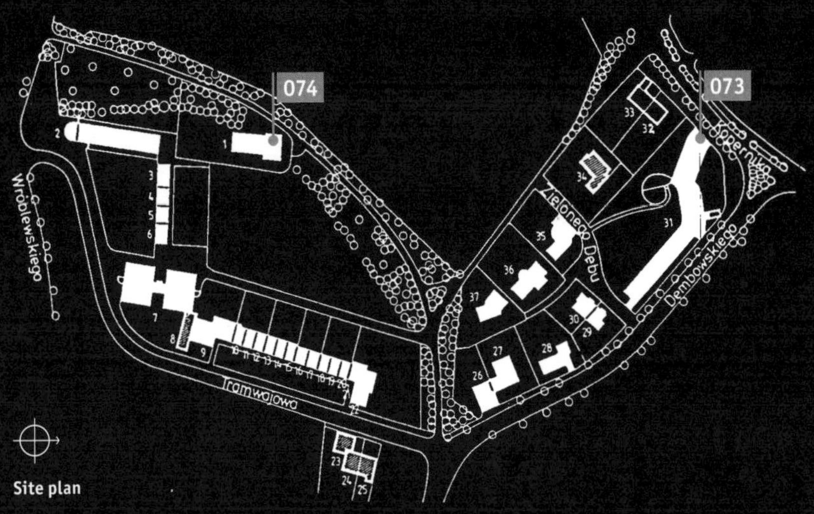

Site plan

1-2	Heim, Kempler	21-27	Effenberger (23–25: not realised)
3-6	Wolf	28	Lange
7-8	Rading (8: not realised)	29-30	Häusler
9	Lange	31	Scharoun
10-12	Moshamer	32-33	Wolf (demolished)
13-15	Lauterbach	34-35	Lauterbach (35: not realised)
16-17	Hadda	36	Hadda
18-20	Häusler	37	Moshamer

Exhibition brochure (1929)

Source: Akademie der Künste, Berlin, Adolf-Rading-Archiv, 50 F. 33

WuWA Model House No. 31

073 C

9 Mikołaja Kopernika Street
Hans Scharoun
1929

The largest building erected as part of the WuWA exhibition was the three-storey Model House No. 31 designed by Hans Scharoun, comprising three wings connected with a diagonal entrance vestibule situated on Kopernika Street. The building was a hotel for the lonely and for childless couples. A one-storey restaurant was created in one of the wings. Above the restaurant, the building featured numerous balconies. A terrace with a garden was created on the roof of the second wing. The apartments occupied the entire depth of the building. When designing the building, the architect was inspired by transoceanic steam ships, hence the round holes in the lateral walls of the building resembling bull's-eyes found on ships. The dynamic form of the building was subordinated to the functions performed by its parts. Ultimately dedicated to white-collar workers, the building combined the function of hotel with independent apartment. Dinners were served in the hotel restaurant, since the apartments were only furnished with a kitchen annex. Today, the Park Hotel and the State Labour Inspectorate are located in the building.

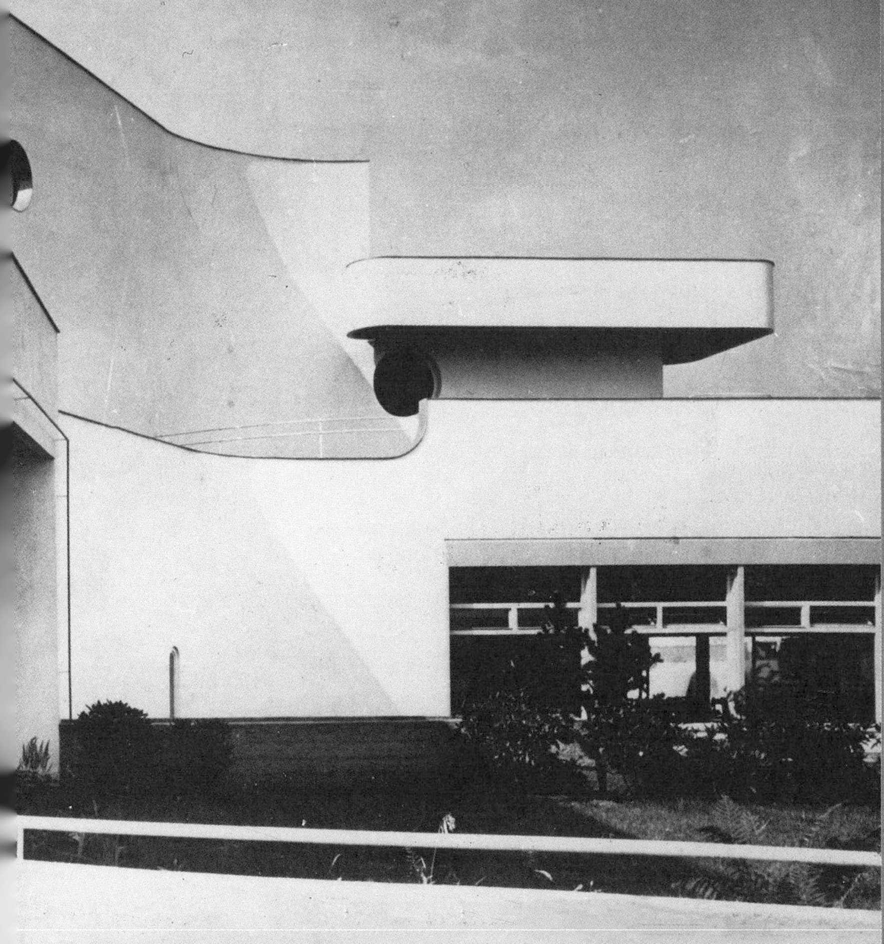

Source: Akademie der Künste, Berlin, Hans-Scharoun-Archiv, 3717 F. 77/30a, F. Klettephoto, Breslau

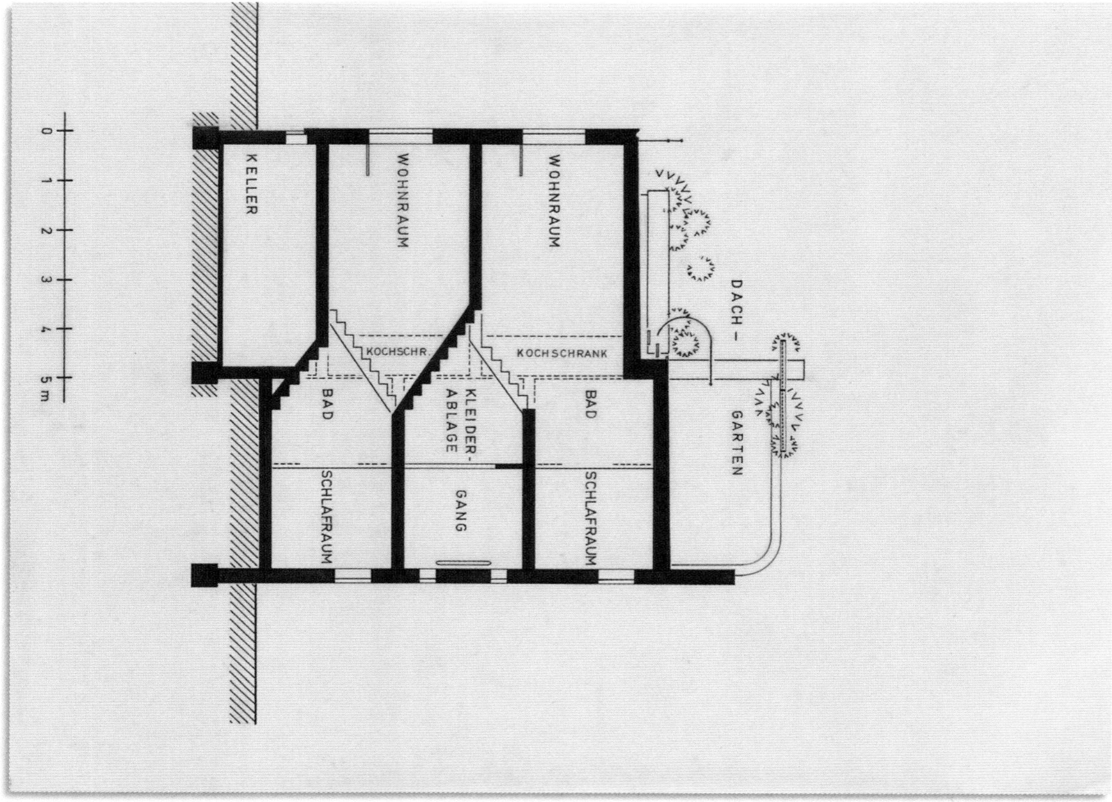

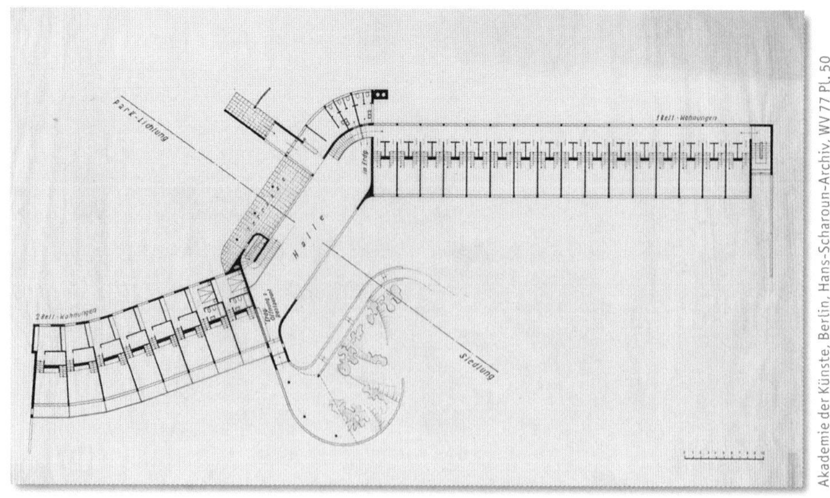

Akademie der Künste, Berlin, Hans-Scharoun-Archiv, WV 77 Pl. 50

DACH–
GARTEN
BAD
SCHLAFRAUM
WOHNRAUM
KOCHSCHRANK
KLEIDER-
ABLAGE
GANG
WOHNRAUM
KOCHSCHR.
BAD
SCHLAFRAUM
KELLER
0 1 2 3 4 5 m

Source: Akademie der Künste, Berlin, Hans-Scharoun-Archiv, WV 77 Pl. 52

Photo: Thomas Michael Krüger

Photo: Thomas Michael Krüger

Photo: Philipp Meuser

WuWA Kindergarten

074 C

18 Zygmunta Wróblewskiego St.
Paul Heim, Albert Kempter (1929)
Maćków Pracownia Projektowa
(reconstruction: 2013–2014)

An innovative Modernist kindergarten for sixty children was built as part of the WuWA exhibition on Wróblewskiego Street (the former Grüneichener Weg) in 1929. The building was designed by Paul Heim and Albert Kempter and included a garden designed by Erich Vergin. The building was created out of prefabricated wooden elements of the Doecker system by Christoph & Unmack A.G. The one-storey building featuring a wooden façade

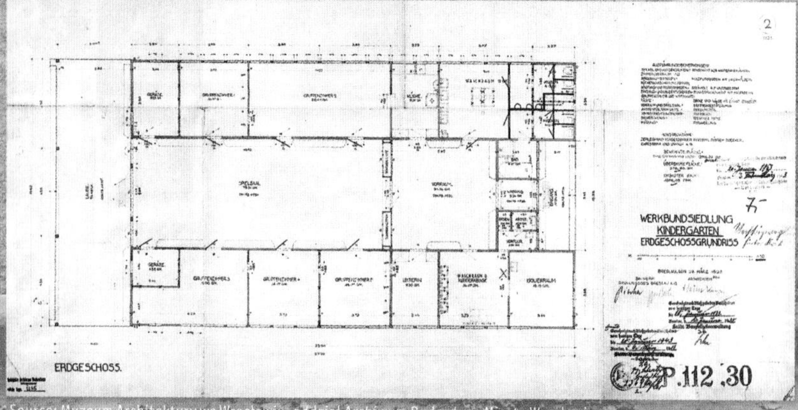

Source: Muzeum Architektury we Wrocławiu, oddział Archiwum Budowlane Miasta Wrocławia

Photo: Jean Molitor

consisted of a large central hall, illuminated by a skylight elevated above the flat roof, and of smaller peripheral rooms. The simple form of the building is complemented by arcades – the entrance arcade and the arcade overlooking the playground. The interiors were furnished with Thonet Mundus furniture. The building which survived both the war and Communist times was consumed by fire on the night of the 6th to the 7th of July 2006. Over the following years, the authorities decided to rebuild it. In June 2012, the President of Wrocław handed the plot over to the Wrocław Chamber of Architects. The reconstruction process commenced in 2013 and was supervised by the Maćków design office. The design outlined the recreation of the original wooden frame of the building. The works, which were co-financed by EU funds, were completed at the beginning of 2014.

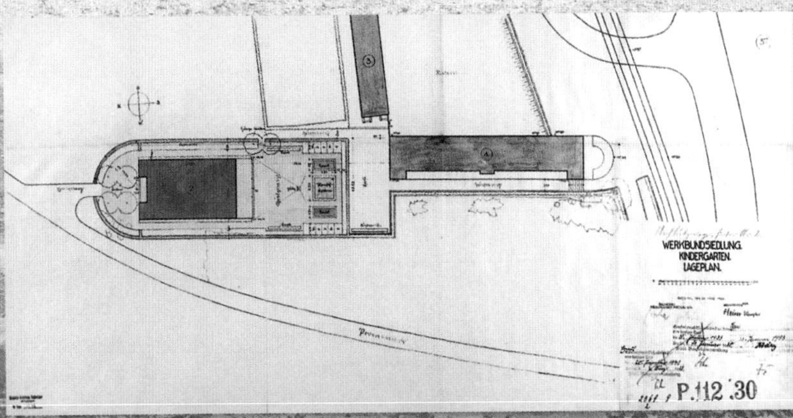

Source: Muzeum Architektury we Wrocławiu, oddział Archiwum Budowlane Miasta Wrocławia

Breslau – Hochhaus (Städt. Sparkasse)
GAZETA
WYBORCZA
Bank Zachodni WBK

Municipal Savings and Credit Union

075 B

Rynek 9/1/
1 Solny Square
Heinrich Rump
1931

In 1928, the city authorities announced a competition for the new venue for the Municipal Savings and Credit Union. The competition was attended by multiple renowned German architects. The jury included Max Berg, the author of the Centennial Hall, among others. The winning design was by Heinrich Rump and assumed two forms: a ten-storey form from Rynek and a seven-storey form from the side of Solny Square. The building was characterised by simplicity and modernity. In the opinion of the competition jury, its modest façade comprising horizontal strips of identical windows matched the space of the market square perfectly. The façade was made of travertine cladding and the last storey was glazed. A paternoster lift was installed in the building. From the side of the market square, the main entrance portico is decorated by convex Art Nouveau high reliefs inspired by Egyptian art. An interpreted coat of arms of Wrocław in the form of defragmented and vertically placed elements is located to the right of the entrance. A proposal for the reconstruction of the building was put forward in the 1940s. Ultimately, the building has survived unchanged and currently houses a commercial bank.

Photo: Philipp Meuser

Photo: Thomas Michael Krüger

Gazeta Wyborcza Journal Venue
076 B
2/3 Solny Square
Adolf Rading, Hans Leistikow
1925–1928

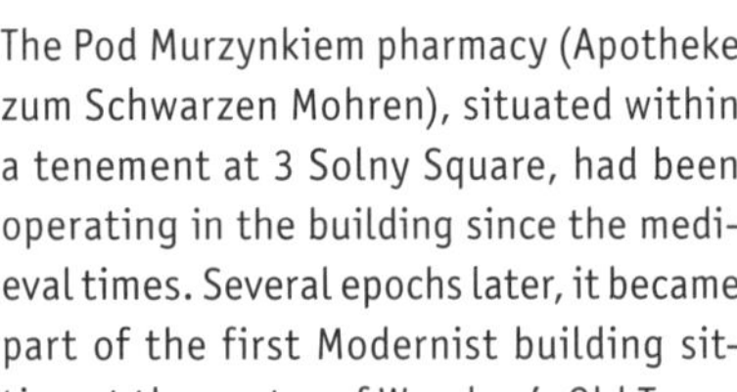

The Pod Murzynkiem pharmacy (Apotheke zum Schwarzen Mohren), situated within a tenement at 3 Solny Square, had been operating in the building since the medieval times. Several epochs later, it became part of the first Modernist building sitting at the centre of Wrocław's Old Town. We owe this change to the brilliant architect Adolf Rading who, between 1925 and 1928, carried out a reconstruction which merged tenements 2 and 3. Firstly, in 1925 Rading modernised the façade of the tenement, reconstructing the entrance to the pharmacy and renovating its interior with the assistance of painter Hans Leistikow. In 1928, he purchased the neighbouring tenement and ordered an architect to connect both buildings. The end result was a six-storey building with a flat roof. The last floor was retracted and terraced.

Source: Akademie der Künste, Berlin (Rading 0038-F-03)

Photo: Philipp Meuser

The façade comprised alternating layers of strips of non-transparent glass cladding and windows separated with black glass walls. The effect produced was one of a strip of glazing, whereas glazing across the entire length of the façade was only applied to the last two storeys of the frame superstructure. Destroyed during the war, the building was gradually reconstructed. However, it was only in the 1990s that the details designed by Rading were fully restored. Currently, the building houses the *Gazeta Wyborcza* journal.

Source: Akademie der Künste, Berlin (Rading 0038-F-02)

Tenement No. 2 ↑ **077 B**

2 Michała Bałuckiego Street
Moritz Hadda (1863), Hadda & Schlesinger (reconstruction: 1922)

The neo-Renaissance residential tenement was erected in 1863 at 2 Bałuckiego Street (the former Agnesstrasse). Its interiors were rebuilt in 1907 for the purpose of establishing a school of music. However, in 1922, the building was acquired by the Karlsruhe Life Insurance Company which ordered the Hadda & Schlesinger architectural company to perform yet another reconstruction. As a result, the façade was changed to reflect Expressionist forms. The design proposed by Hadda, a student of Hans Poelzig, the author of Model House No. 36 erected for the purposes of the WuWA exhibition, referred to Expressionist forms and resulted from the functional use of specific spatial solutions. Prismatic walls and inclinations shaping the texture of the façade fulfilled an important role in illuminating the interiors. The building's interesting aesthetic effect was reinforced by the zigzag peaks of the façade. The building survived World War II in ideal condition and can be still admired in unchanged form.

Photo: Thomas Michael Krüger

Photo: Philipp Meuser

Main Post Office ← 078 B
1 Zygmunta Krasińskiego Street
Lothar Neumann
1926–1929

The management of Polish Post purchased a construction plot for the new Postal Check Office (German: Postscheckamt) in 1925. Due to the marshy texture of its soil, the works commenced with the hammering of 2,000 concrete piles which serve as a foundation for the new building. The design proposed by Lothar Neumann outlined the construction of a monumental high-rise. Completed in 1929, the building consisted of eleven storeys and was 43 m tall, including two internal yards and referring to the post office in the Berlin Kreuzberg district. Maintained in the style of Late German Expressionism, the building boasting a 142 m long frontage was decorated by Gothic ornaments. The façades were lined with dark red brick finished with bas-reliefs and cartouches presenting scenes from the lives of city residents and the history of post since 1590. A garden was placed on the roof. Damaged in the siege of Wrocław in 1945, the building was reconstructed in 1950 and was taken over by the Wrocław 1 post office. Afterwards, the building would also house the Office of the Registrar, a worker hotel and an outpatient clinic. Since 1956, the building has housed the Museum of Post and Telecommunications.

Southern Hydroelectric Power Plant ↑ 079 B
46 Nowy Świat Street
Max Berg
1921–1924

A hydroelectric power plant was planned in this location where the water mills used to stand as early as the end of the nineteenth century. In 1916, the city purchased two plots featuring two devastated mills, but was ready to commence works only in 1921. The first of the two power plants was erected according to Max Berg's design. The building comprises a horizontal machine room with reinforced concrete frame structure filled with brick and a vertical control room. The structure was designed by engineer Günther Trauer, the subsequent construction adviser for the city of Wrocław. The masonry buildings were decorated by extensive visual elements, including a granite supraport above the entrance portal with a bas-relief of a naked man emerging from water, sculpted by Robert Bednorz; a metalwork by Jaroslav Vonka and the Wrocław coat of arms, created by Hans Leistikow. The power plant survived World War II without major damage and was reopened in 1945. In 1948, it was handed over to the Energy Co-op. In the 1960s, the complex underwent reconstruction, and two new turbines were commissioned in 1970. The power plant continues to operate today.

079 B

Photo: Jean Molitor

Photo: Jean Molitor

Northern Hydroelectric Power Plant ↑ **080 B**

1 Zygmunta Krasińskiego Street

Max Berg

1924–1925

An element of the Municipal Water Barrage incorporated into the downtown water node, the flow-type Northern Power Plant was commissioned in January 1926. In common with the Southern Power Plant, the building was designed by Max Berg, Its interior design was proposed by Ludwig Mashamer, and Professor Jaroslav Vonka was in charge of the metalworks and the ornamental entry door. The first works on the building, which was erected in the place of a scorched mill (Werdermühle), commenced in March 1924. The reinforced concrete structure of this simple Modernist building was covered by a masonry façade. A weir – initially permanent – with a pile-stone structure is situated next to the power plant. In 1942, it was replaced with an electrical flap weir. Although the Northern Power Plant was listed in the register of monuments on 10 August 1993, it has never ceased to fulfill its function. The historical Mieszczańska Sluice, erected in 1974 out of wood and reconstructed to create a masonry structure between 1874 and 1879, is located near the power plant. Destroyed during World War II, the power plant was rebuilt between 1991 and 2000 and is used for various sporting events.

Banquet Pavilion ↓ **081 A**

8 Wojciecha z Brudzewa Street

Max Tauber

1929

The Modernist pavilion designed by Max Tauber, completed in 1929, refers to the concept of organic design propagated by Hugo Häring. Hence the building situated close to the river, serving as a residence of the Association for Life and Treatment and resembling a steam boat by shape. Erected near the border of the Szczytnicki Park, the building comprised a part of a much larger recreational complex including, among other things, sports courts, tennis courts and swimming pools. The building with the flat roof consists of a two-storey frontage erected on a rectangular floor plan housing the administrative part, the central part housing a restaurant (built on a spindle floor plan

Photo: Jean Molitor

Photo: Jean Molitor

with rounded ends) and a roofed terrace protruding towards the River Odra. The façade consists of strips of windows, while the structure of the building is partially wooden and partially masonry. The façade was covered with wooden cladding. After the war, the building, which served as a caféteria for the Medical Academy, was renovated and extended several times in a chaotic manner which departed considerably from the original vision. During the 1990s, the building served as a banquet hall. Fortunately, the building has recently undergone a general renovation, restoring it to its original splendour and reinstituting it as one of the icons of Wrocław Modernism.

New Headquarters Building ↑ 082 A

126 Gajowicka Street
Otto Rudolf Salvisberg
1929

Erected in 1929, this massive Modernist edifice designed by the Swiss architect Otto Rudolf Salvisberg was situated in the southern part of the city within a quarter enclosed by the streets Pretficza, Gajowicka, Sztabowa and Łączności. The entire construction process took only eighty-five days. The end result was a flat-roofed, three-winged building with a five-storey structure parallel to Gajowicka Street, as well as two three-storey wings. The symmetry of this very simple form

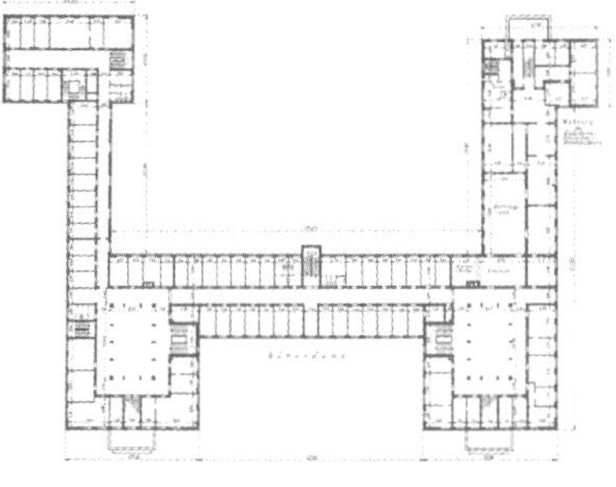

is emphasised by two stacks. The façade is lined with red brick and windows were placed in two even strips, owing to which the façade emphasised the horizontal composition of the building. The raw edifice was devoid of nearly all decorative elements, with the exception of entrances. During the siege of Wrocław, the entire neighbourhood was nearly entirely destroyed, whereas the Salvisberg building had endured nearly intact, together with its nearest vicinity – the paved paths and the greenery. In 1945, the building erected as the residence of the VIII Silesian Reichswehr Army Corps was taken over by the Red Army, to be finally acquired by the Polish Army headquarters. For many years, the building housed the command and staff of the Silesian Military Precinct. Since 2011, the building has been the venue of the IV Regional Logistics Base. In 1973, a ceramic eagle sculpture by Tadeusz Teller was placed on the base of the former German *Landswehr* monument.

City Lavatory ↓

083 C

1 Marii Curie-Skłodowskiej St.
Max Berg, Albert Kempter
1914

The decision to build a city lavatory was made in 1912. Due to the shape of the plot, Max Berg designed a building with front façades on the V-shaped floor plan and a rounded corner containing a Modernist, elliptical staircase devoid of nearly any decorations. Completed in 1914, the five-storey building with a reinforced concrete frame structure filled with brick and prefabricated concrete panels (a staircase) included a small internal yard and a gable roof. A bas-relief sculpted by Alfred Vocke, presenting bathing people, a woman with a child and a tax collector, was placed above the entrance door. From the side of Maria Skłodowska-Curie Street, the façade consists of fifteen window per floor which are grouped into three and separated by lesenes. A spherical curved roof was built above the staircase. The building survived the siege of Wrocław and functioned nearly unchanged until the 1980s. In 1993, the building was entered to the list of monuments and its interiors were constructed to serve the function of an office.

Photo: Bartek Barczyk

Source: iStock (Mariusz Szczygieł)

Sępolno Estate ↑ 084 A

The streets Dębowskiego, Monte Cassino, Mickiewicza, 9 Maja

Hermann Wahlich, Paul Heim, Albert Kempter, Hugo Althoff

1919–1935

The Zimpeln 1 estate, referring to the Garden City concept, was executed in several stages (within the course of more than a dozen years) in an area where the first settlements had been established as early as the thirteenth century. The first stage, the northern part – enclosed by the streets of Adama Mickiewicza, 9 Maja and Kosynierów Górskich – comprised two-storey, multi-family buildings covered with gable roofs and was completed in 1925. The buildings designed by Wahlich and Heim reflected the English design style and a simplified Prussian Classicism. The next stage was the 1930 row development with an offset containing a gateway, situated upon 9 Maja Street, which was designed by Heim and Albert Kempter. With its characteristic, triangular bays accentuating the avant-corps of the staircases, this part of the development referred to Expressionism, although acquired certain International Style features through the use of a flat roof. The entire complex adopts the shape of an eagle when viewed from above. A Modernist building of the Friedrich Ebert Folk School (the current Primary School No. 45) designed by Hugo Althoff was built in 1928 on the western side of the current Powstańców Warszawskich Square. The arched form of the masonry building was characterised by a colonnade and outstanding white window carpentry. In 1933, a church designed by Kempter, with a Cubist tower, was built on the eastern side of the square. The estate was completed in 1935. The Sępolno Estate survived the war and the siege of the Tower of Wrocław.

Ołtaszyn Estate
085 A
Strączkowa Street
Ernst May
1921

In 1921, an estate was built for farm workers, referred to by its residents as Kozi Park (Goat Park). The estate was designed by the German architect and urban planner Ernst May and consisted of thirty-six twin multi-family houses with gardens running along an internal street and a square yard intended for children. The entire complex included a total of 150 flats. The buildings were built at the lowest expense – hence the use of a large curved roof of 5 m. Entrances and windows were installed in the end walls. In turn, there were only four small windows facing the side of the street. A kitchen and a room were situated on each floor. Each building had a toilet with a feces box, a shaft for kitchen wastewater and a well. May was inspired by English garden suburbs when designing the estate. He applied the concept of a functional kitchen draft, which is used until the present day, in his projects. The estate survived World War II and can be still admired in its unchanged form.

Photo: Philipp Meuser

Photo: Stanisław Klimek

Photo: Philipp Meuser

Photo: Philipp Meuser

Modernist Księże Małe Estate 086 A

The streets Opolska, Bytomska, Górnośląska, Tarnogórska
Paul Heim, Albert Kempter
1928–1930

The term *Existenzminimum* (Minimal Existence) was developed during the interwar period. This development type was to respond to human needs while providing an economy of solutions. One of the examples testifying to such an approach is the Modernist worker estate in Księże Małe (Klein Tschanch) which refers to the Bauhaus programme. It is situated in the southwestern part of the Krzyki district and was designed by Paul Heim and Albert Kempter. This 12 ha estate intended for 3,000 people was erected in almost a year at the order of the Wrocław S.A. Estate Company. The development consisted of long rows of masonry houses covered with flat roofs featuring prominent eaves. The thick-grained plaster façades of particular buildings differed in terms of the bays, arcade layouts and the rhythm of windows and balconies. The estate includes, among other things, shops, a kindergarten, an assembly hall and a boiler room with a bathhouse and a laundry room. All internal yards were planted with greenery. The layout of the houses at the southern and northern ends of the streets is L-shaped to close up the internal space of the estate. To enable easy recognition of particular buildings, ceramic bas-reliefs with animal motifs were placed above the entrances. In 1996, the Księże Małe Estate was recorded in the register of monuments owing to its "outstanding achievements of Modernist urban design".

Photo: Stanisław Klimek

Westend Estate
Słubicka Street
Theo Effenberger,
Heinrich Lauterbach
1924–1930

087 A

Between 1924 and 1930, a Modernist estate, Siedlung Westend, was built in the Przedmieście Mikołajskie area (the former Nicolai Vorstadt). The urban layout of this region was determined in the middle of the nineteenth century and initially adopted a geometric street arrangement. However, at the beginning of the twentieth century this urban layout was modified to add certain picturesque features. Two estates were therefore created: the Westend estate as well as the neighbouring Viehreiche estate, which was completely destroyed during World War II. The preserved Westend development consisted of small masonry buildings featuring various forms and modest details, maintained in a Modernist and Expressionist style. The school complex (building no. 1) is the architectural dominant of the estate. The complex was erected in 1914, according to a design by Fritz Behrendt, on the axis of Główna Street. The complex separates a row of buildings designed by Theo Effenberger from those designed by Heinrich Lauterbach. After the war, despite the nearby battle of Festung Breslau, the salvaged estate development was successfully completed. One of its most noteworthy elements, despite its poor condition, is the building at the corner of the streets Słubicka and Zgorzelecka, probably designed by Witold Molicki, and reflecting the Modernist style of the inter-war period. Today, the estate is marred by the appearance of numerous garages built in the vicinity of the salvaged buildings.

All photos: Philipp Meuser

Former Na Polance Estate
Na Polance Street
Heinrich Lauterbach
1938–1939

088 A

Just before the outburst of World War II, the authorities planned to build eight houses perpendicularly to the river between Na Polance (the former Polinke Weg) and Piesza Street. Ultimately, only three blocks of flats were erected according to a design by Heinrich Lauterbach, a student of Hans Poelzig and the author of the concept behind the entire estate. Although created in a period when the Traditionalist architecture reflecting historical models, as promoted by the Nazis, was a dominant feature, the buildings were constructed according to a design referring to the "rotten inter-war avant-garde". Simple T-shape forms, although covered with gable roofs, were perfectly incorporated into the environment. The southern, taller building apexes with spacious loggias were clearly accentuated. All apartments were furnished with bathrooms. Situated on the eastern side of the buildings, the entrances to staircases with their round windows were decorated with brick cladding. Green yards were established inbetween particular buildings. The three blocks built in the 1990s on the western side of the estate are in keeping with the pre-war urban concept proposed by Lauterbach.

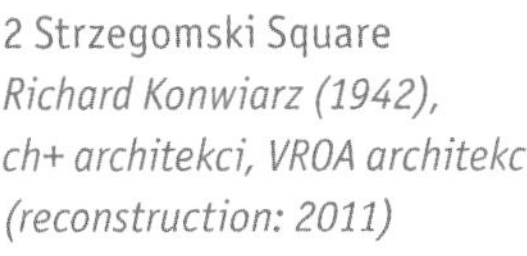

Wrocław Contemporary Museum
2 Strzegomski Square
Richard Konwiarz (1942), ch+ architekci, VROA architekci (reconstruction: 2011)

089 A

During World War II, four above-ground air-raid shelters designed by the architect Richard Konwiarz – who had cooperated, among others, with Max Berg before the war – were built in Wrocław. All structures erected between 1940 and 1943 referred to Late Classicist architecture. The six-storey free-standing shelter building on a circular floor plan on Strzegomski Square has reinforced concrete walls, 1.1 m thick, and 1.5 m ceilings. The façade of this cylindrical building with two rectangular annexes and a cylindrical top is decorated with inter-storey cornices. During the war, the eastern façade with the bossage was ornamented with a fascist eagle. The interior of the building includes a staircase connecting the circular and radial corridors leading to small rooms. In 1945, the shelter served as a fortress hospital (Festunglazaret II) and a resistance point. After the war, it served various functions and housed, among other things, warehouses, stores, and even a pub. Ultimately, after it was renovated in 2011 the shelter became the venue of the Wrocław Contemporary Museum.

Olympic Stadium ↑ **090 A**

18 Ignacego Jana
Paderewskiego Alley
Richard Konwiarz
1926–1928

This multi-functional stadium was also referred to as the Olympic Stadium, probably due to the fact that its designer, Richard Konwiarz, was a double Olympic medal winner in architecture (1928, Amsterdam and 1932, Los Angeles). The stadium was the central part of the sports complex built between 1926 and 1928 in the elevated Wrocław Zalesie district. Initially, the stadium would accommodate 35,000 spectators in an above-ground non-roofed auditorium. In 1938, the extension of the Zalesie Sports Park featuring the stadium, also supervised by Richard Konwiarz, was completed. The stadium received a reinforced concrete auditorium; a red masonry façade and a monumental clock tower with a belfry. The entire structure referred to the architecture of the Olympic Stadium in Berlin, reflecting the Third Reich style. One of the spectators attending the 1938 propaganda sports competition held at the Hermann Göring Stadium was Adolf Hilter himself, who visited Wrocław at the time. Severely damaged during the siege of the city, the complex was renovated after the war and successively extended afterwards. In the 1970s, the building was handed over to the Physical Education Academy. In 1978, four lighting masts of 80 m were installed around the stadium and a heated playing field was set up. In 2006, the city purchased the complex from the Academy.

Regional Police Headquarters **091 B**

31-33 Podwale Street
Rudolf Fernholz
1926–1928

This monumental edifice, designed by Fernholz, was erected in the area of a former garden belonging to a Silesian merchant to become the headquarters of the Police Presidium. To reinforce the area, more than 2,500 concrete piles were poured under the building as a foundation. The five-storey building had five internal yards and occupied the quarter enclosed by the streets of Franciszka Druckiego-Lubeckiego, Podwale, Łąkowa and Muzealna. The main entrance within the most representative façade facing Podwale Street

Source: iStock (Mariusz Szczygiel)

is decorated by a portico with four pillars of more than 13 m. Each of them is crowned with a sculpture presenting a Roman warrior, created by Feliks Kupsch. The façade of the building is covered with blue-violet clinker cladding. Apart from police headquarters, the building also housed a custody centre and flats for the employees, including an apartment for the Chief of Police. The innovative design was furnished, among other things, with two telephone switchboards, elevators and fire sensors. Building interiors have been maintained in the Art Déco style. The impressive lobby was finished with malachite glazed ceramics. The building survived the siege of Wrocław and housed the Communist Security Office (UB) between the period encompassing the years from 1945 to 1956. At present this imposing building is occupied by regional police headquarters.

Photo: Philipp Meuser

Voivodeship Office 092 B

1 Powstańców Warszawy Square

Feliks Bräuler

1939–1945

The first competition to design the new venue of the Wrocław authorities was announced in 1927. The winning design was proposed by Alexander Müller and Ferdinand Schmidt. Ultimately, due to the lack of funding, the investment was abandoned. Although the next competition announced by the city authorities was closed by selecting Erwin Grau's design, the construction of the building only commenced in 1939 according to a design by the state construction adviser Feliks Bräuler. It is interesting to note that construction works were conducted even during the siege of the city in 1945. This masonry three-storey building with a usable attic, consisting of six wings surrounded by internal yards, was covered with a gable, flattened roof. The interior contains six symmetrically distributed staircases. A two-storey voivodeship assembly hall is situated in the south-western part of the building. The arched roof was adapted to the curve of the River Odra. Acording to Werner Maech's design, the building was to enclose the new Nazi Wrocław development from the northeast. Significantly damaged during the siege of the city, the building was reconstructed after the war, including its façade. Today, it houses the voivodeship office.

Photo: Philipp Meuser

1200–1850
1850–1945
1945–1989
1990–2015

Photo: Philipp Meuser

Kościuszko Residential Estate 093 B

Kościuszko Square, the streets Świdnicka and Kościuszki
Roman Tunikowski
1954–1958

Kościuszki Square, together with its neighbouring development, is the architectural salon of the city as well as its central point. It is modelled on Parisian designs such as the Vendôme and other royal squares. Prior to World War II, the square had been a monument for the Prussian General Friedrich Bogislav von Tauentzien. Unfortunately, the development and the layout of the square were nearly completely destroyed during the siege of Wrocław. The extent of the damage to the city was so severe that the reconstruction of the square commenced a decade after the end of the war. In 1945, a team of architects of the Wrocław Miastoprojekt office were assigned the task to reconstruct the representative Tadeusza Kościuszki Square and its entire development. The line of development of the Kościuszko residential estate built between 1954 and 1958 was modelled upon the original layout of the square. The façade of the five-storey Classicist masonry buildings covered with steep roofs was lined with sandstone. Their compositions were a reference to the former Dresden Bank. In the section between Kościuszki Square and the junction of the streets Świdnicka and Piłsudskiego, the designers planned arcades featuring decorative chandeliers. With time, the façades of the buildings were successfully filled with neon lights. In 1994, the residential complex designed by Tunikowski was entered to the register of monuments as part of an urban complex.

Photo: Philipp Meuser

Photo: Philipp Meuser

Manhattan (Grunwaldzki Square Estate)

094 C

Grunwaldzki Square
Jadwiga Grabowska-Hawrylak
1967–1973

Comprising six multi-family residential buildings and three commercial pavilions, the complex was built upon Grunwaldzki Square in adherence to an avant-garde design created by the renowned architect Jadwiga Grabowska-Hawrylak. The complex was completed and commissioned in 1973. The design outlined the construction of six 55 m high-rises covered with white plaster and clinker brick upon a concrete platform. Plants seeded in dedicated planters were to climb on the balconies clad in wood and rounded cavities in the façade. In turn, the flat roofs of the commercial pavilions were to be covered with gardens. Unfortunately, due to investment cost cuts, the façade was not finished and the buildings acquired a Brutalist character. The plants were not seeded on the roofs of the pavilions – hence the 1974 SARP Award for the complex, also referred to as the Wrocław Manhattan. The buildings are included in the regional register of monuments.

In recent years, the Jednostka Architektury foundation has prepared a thermal insulation design for the buildings in cooperation with the designer of the estate. Unfortunately, as a result of the renovation the buildings have lost a part of their unique character.

Source: Filip Springer Archive

094 C

Source: Filip Springer Archive

All photos: Filip Springer

094 C

Rotunda with the Racławice Panorama

095 B

11 Purkyniego Street
Ewa Dziekońska, Marek Dziekoński
1966–1985

The building was erected as exhibition space to showcase a rotating hyperboloid panoramic painting commemorating the victorious battle of Racławice, painted in Lviv under the supervision of Wojciech Kossak and Jan Styka. Announced in 1956, the competition for the design of this building in its current location was closed by selecting the concept put forward by Ewa Dziekońska and Marek Dziekoński. However, for political reasons, the raw building was commissioned as late as 1967. Due to the shortage of funding, further works were withheld. Thanks to pressure exerted by the Social Committee for the Racławice Panorama, established in 1980 and headed by Professor Alfred Jahn, the building was completed in 1985. The structure, consisting of a rotunda expanding towards the top, rests on prefabricated concrete load-bearing columns. It is connected with a tunnel ramp featuring the entrance part which houses ticket offices and cloakrooms. The walls of the building comprise wedge-shaped modules. It is covered with a glass roof. Traces of formwork can be found upon the raw concrete façade. An excellent example of Brutalist architecture, the building was listed in the register of monuments in 1996.

All photos: Philipp Meuser

Trzonolinowiec **096 B**
76 Kościuszki Street
Jacek Burzyński, Andrzej Skorupa
1961–1967

In the year 1967, the corner of the streets Kościuszki and Dworcowa was enriched with a unique experimental high-rise designed by Jacek Burzyński and Andrzej Skorupa. The innovative structure of the building consisted of a concrete core, transferring all compressive loads to the foundations, whereby all ceilings have been suspended on steel lines. All storeys of the building hung on twelve lines fastened to the tip of the core and were anchored at ground floor level to make the structure more rigid. Ceiling suspension therefore commenced with the highest floors. Stunning owing to its slim form, this modern edifice with its first level suspended several metres above ground was awarded the *1967 Building of the Year* title. The building housed forty-one spacious apartments furnished with state-of-the-art technologies, including floor heating. Unfortunately, after a few years it was discovered that the ceilings of the building would hover under the influence of wind which caused partition walls and shield ceilings to crack. The building was put out of service and reconstructed according to a design proposed by the engineers of the Wrocław University of Technology, who created a nearly typical frame structure and changed the façade by replacing the window strips with common windows which entirely destroyed the original concept by Burzyński and Skorupa. The building was recommissioned in 1974. For years, it has been occupied by actors of Wrocław-based theatres.

DOLMED 097 A

40 Legnicka Street

Anna Tarnawska, Jerzy Tarnawski

1974–1977

One of the most innovative health centres in Central Eastern Europe was commissioned in 1977. This icon of the High-Tech trend was designed by Anna and Jerzy Tarnowscy, the authors of numerous buildings created during this period for the Wrocław Elwro computer factory. This free-standing three-storey building featuring an aluminium façade manufactured in Italy was not only furnished with the most innovative equipment, but was also elegantly finished. The tower housing the staircase was covered with a golden stained glass mosaic, whereas the interiors were lined with granite and marble. One of the most important elements was the environment designed with the patients' and employees' comfort in mind, consisting of lawns, terraces and a fountain. The futurist interior was also recurrently used as a film and television location. Unfortunately, with time the ambient of the building gradually deteriorated, and the elements proposed by the designers were replaced by car parks. In 2013, the building was thoroughly renovated, and the interiors reconstructed to provide space for the growing number of patients.

Chemistry Auditorium **098** **B**

14 Fryderyka Joliot-Curie Street
Marian Barski, Krystyna Barska
1970–1971

In 1964, SARP (Association of Polish Architects) organised a competition for developing Grunwaldzki Square to accommodate the buildings housing the Institute of Chemistry and Mathematics. One of the elements of the building complex is the Chemistry Auditorium, built according to a design by Marian Barski and Krystyna Barska. The lower part of the two-storey building, preceded by a terrace overlooking the Odra River, is retracted. The glass façade of the building, combined with incredibly innovative and elegantly finished interiors, creates an impressive and still ultra-modern building. The design was characterised by enormous care for architectural detail. The floor of the lobby located on the ground floor was made of granite, and the ceilings covered in wooden cladding with a hidden lighting installation. Ramps leading to the second floor are lined with coarse terrazzo. The walls of the auditoriums are entirely covered with wood, and the suspended ceiling consists of pyramid elements. The columns are finished with terracotta with a black and white chessboard pattern. Interiors of the complex are dominated by grey which is mixed with colourful detail. The design proposed not only lighting and furniture, but additionally the smallest details, such as door handles, hangers, or even radiator shields. The designers thus drew inspiration for the auditorium from the masters of modern architecture. A reverse cone for collecting rainwater was placed in front of the building, while a similar solution was applied by Corbusier in his Notre-Dame du Haut. This unique example of post-war Modernism was put out of use by the University in the year 2007 and would deteriorate afterwards, serving as storage for rubbish. Fortunately, in 2012, the building was subsequently listed in the register of architectural monuments.

All photos: Philipp Meuser

Source: iStock (Mariusz Szczygiel)

Pencil and Crayon Dormitories 099 C

30 Grunwaldzki Square

Marian Barski, Krystyna Barska

1989–1991

The design for the University of Wrocław dormitories by Marian and Krystyna Barski was created in the year 1985. The twin high-rises of 19 m and 23 m were erected on a shared base between 1989 and 1991. The Modernist form of the reinforced concrete buildings surprises with its slender shape and a steep gable roof, thanks to which the buildings resemble a pencil and a crayon – hence their names. Both buildings feature prominent glazed first floors housing auxiliary functions, such as a gym, a television room and students' club. In 1992, the project won the second degree award of the Ministry of Construction and Spatial Management. For years, the Crayon dormitory was the tallest building in Wrocław. Housing more than 800 people, although created in a period of economic crisis, the buildings served as an example of functional and modern architecture. In 2013, Miastoprojekt Wrocław renovated the façade of the buildings and reconstructed the suspended ceiling.

Galeriowiec

100 A

133-135 Grabiszyńska Street
Stefan Müller
1966–1967

Photo: Philipp Meuser

The construction of this residential and commercial building on Grabiszyńska Street, constituting part of the Gajowice estate built as of 1960 in the south of Wrocław, was completed in 1967. The author of the 1983 design of this nine-storey Modernist building was Stefan Müller, an excellent architect, visionary and creator of the Terra X global urban complex proposing the transfer of human activity to a load-bearing structure placed 2 km above the face of the entire planet. Müller organised two *International Exhibitions of Intentional Architecture*: *Terra 1* (1975) and *Terra 2* (1981). A characteristic feature of the building on Grabiszyńska Street, housing 120 apartments, was its black and white façade resembling a chessboard and consisting of geometric forms. In turn, the façade was dominated by two modern, symmetrical and nearly entirely glazed staircases. Unfortunately, now dirty and deserted, the form of the building is nothing like the modern, metropolitan structure proposed by Müller.

Photo: Philipp Meuser

Photo: Philipp Meuser

ZETO ↑ 101 B

7-13 Ofiar Oświęcimskich Street
Anna Tarnawska, Jerzy Tarnawski
1965–1969

Developed by Miastoprojekt, the concept behind a venue for the oldest Polish IT company proposed the construction of a simple three-storey reinforced concrete edifice with glazed corners, built on a square floor plan and retracted with reference to the main frontage towards the street. A patio with a terrace was designed in the central part of the building. Its smooth façade – nearly entirely glazed thanks to the use of window strips in aluminium metalwork – exhibited interiors accommodating innovative calculation devices. The front façade was accentuated with a slanted canopy resting on a wall decorated with round elements. The façade facing Kazimierza Wielkiego Street is adorned with a belt of mosaic Op-Art ornamentation. Decorated in 1969, the building was created on the site of a prewar tenement which used to house the Oscar Giesser mineral water store and wholesale depot. The new building in turn ignited controversy since the designers were accused of breaking the mould of the historical Old Town development. Today, although recognised by both architectural experts and art historians, this neglected building has continued to ignite extreme emotions among its occupants.

Buildings Nos. 4 to 8 (Triplets) ↘ 102 C

4 Mikołaja Reja Street
Maria Molicka
1965–1969

The construction of this complex of three eleven-storey residential buildings designed by Maria Molicka was completed in 1969. These buildings featuring simple forms and minimalist architectural details impressed with the composition of the white façades, the rhythm of which was marked by geometrical flecks of colour (apart from the windows and porte-fenêtres). The entrance part was emphasised by retracting the external staircase wall across the height of the buildings. These were created at the request of the Industrial Construction Company and were erected as a multi-block complex – thus considerably lowering the overall costs tied to the project. Molicka's design became a prototype for a series of buildings erected afterwards, such as, for instance within the Grabiszyńska Street area. The building complex received the prestigious title of *Mister of Wrocław* in 1968. Unfortunately, the abstract façade form of this building was destroyed by the hideous thermal insulation, distorting the original division of the façade. This fate was unfortunately shared by numerous other buildings dating back to the same period.

Photo: Masako Tomokiyo

Mezonetowiec ↑ 103 B

9-12 Kołłątaja Street

Jadwiga Grabowska-Hawrylak, Edmund Frąckiewicz, Maria Tawryczewska, Igor Tawryczewski

1958–1960

Erected upon a narrow plot on Kołłątaja Street during 1960, this free-standing Modernist building was Poland's first gallery house with two-level apartments of 70 m². The apartments consisted of a living room with a terrace, a kitchen annex and a dining room at entrance level, as well as a bathroom, a toilet and two bedrooms on the second level. Horizontal access systems were placed inside the building on every second level, whereas the glazed staircases were placed outside the main outline of the extended quadratic prismatic building. Prefabricated autoclaved aerated concrete elements were used to construct the load-bearing walls of the building. The glazed ground floor was dedicated to services, while a generally accessible terrace was placed on the roof. The concrete façade clearly marks residential modules. Inspired by Le Corbusier's works, the building was published in *L'Architecture d'Aujourd'hui*. Individually renovated by the residents, the loggias have been repainted on a recurring basis which distorted the initial colour concept of the façade.

Photo: Bartek Barczyk

HUTMEN S.A. **104 A**

241 Grabiszyńska Street
Jerzy Surma
1964–1970

Erected between 1964 and 1970 in Grabiszyn, the industrial district of the city, the main production hall of the then Hutmen Independent Medal Metallurgical Processing Plant was designed by Jerzy Surma. The building was erected in the area of the former German Schaefer & Schael metallurgical company, operating in this place up to 1945. The form of this Modernist hall, built on an extended rectangular floor plan, is covered by a characteristic saw-tooth roof. The curve of the roof is reflected in the divisions of the façade on the side facing Grabiszyńska Street, creating a dynamic composition of triangular glazing and concrete cladding. A two-storey administrative building adjoins the hall building. Between 1968 and 1972, the plant was extended to include successive production halls. An outdoor sculpture entitled *Jagusia*, designed by the renowned artist Tadeusz Teller, was placed in front of the entrance to the building. The sculpture presenting a female body was created by the employees of the plant in 1974 as a public contribution. In 2009, the building and the sculpture were recorded on the list of post-war monuments of the city. In spite of this, there have been recent rumours regarding plans to reconstruct the area.

Primary School No. 71 **105 B**

57 Podwale Street
Jadwiga Grabowska-Hawrylak
1959–1960

The majority of schools built as part of the project featuring the slogan "A thousand schools for the thousandth anniversary of the Polish State" were created during the period of ubiquitous Socialist Realism in architecture; all of them looked similar. Exceptions did take place though. One of them was the Leon Kruczkowski Primary School designed by Jadwiga Grabowska-Hawrylak. The founder of the building completed in 1960 was the local Co-op. The complex consists of three different buildings of varying height, covered with flat roofs. The long, two-storey pavilion situated upon Podwale Street housed a caféteria, a library as well as administrative offices. Lecture halls were situated in the perpendicular three-storey building connected to the gym. Together with the façade strips, the exposed structural frame elements emphasised by black terrazzo created a specific rhythm. The composition of the façade was completed by sub-window elements made of white marbelite manufactured in the Wałbrzych glass mill. A gentle ramp running along the façade of the building leads to the main entrance. With time, due to financial problems, the building gradually lost its initial appearance in the course of successive renovations.

All photos: Philipp Meuser

Romanesque House

106 B

8 Nankiera Street
Henryk Dziurla
1966–1969

In 1959, Tadeusz Kozaczewski discovered fragments of a thirteenth-century two-storey Romanesque residential building serving as a venue for the Trzebnica Cistercian Order below Nankiera Street. The structures preserved included two vaulted rooms and a simple hall. Between 1966 and 1969, the building was partially recreated according to a design by Henryk Dziurla. As part of the conservation works, original fragments of the House of the Trzebnica Maidens were unveiled, such as the barrel vault preserved in the lower part of the building. The ceiling was removed in part of the building and the complex in its entirety was covered with a modern reinforced concrete ceiling, thus creating an interesting exhibition pavilion. The front façade was furnished with a glazed structure, providing an insight into the interior of the building housing the Lower Silesian Photography Centre, a division of the Art and Culture Centre in Wrocław. The building was enlarged in the year 1996 by adding a third glazed room featuring a mezzanine.

Nurse Dormitory of the Medical Academy

107 A

88-96 Ślężna Street
Marian Barski, Krystyna Barska
1985

A closed competition to design a building complex for the Medical Academy, announced in 1975, was completed by selecting a concept proposed by Krystyna Barska and Marian Barski. One element of the design was the complex of three unique nurse dormitories completed in 1985. The form of these flat-roofed buildings of varying height, spanning three to nine storeys, is dynamised by their façade. The terrace effect was magnified by the concept of diagonally terminated loggias (one for each apartment within the building) as well as properly selected window carpentry. Unfortunately, the buildings were neglected and fell into demise. Their residents changed windows and modified the balconies which made the buildings lose their architectural cohesion. Later sold by the Medical Academy, the buildings ceased to serve as a nurse dormitory in 2012. The environment surrounding the complex, overgrown with gas stations and sheet metal supermarkets, has nothing in common with this self-sufficient community-oriented mini-estate.

All photos: Philipp Meuser

Nowy Targ Square **108** B

Nowy Targ Square

Włodzimierz Czerechowski, Ryszard Natuszewicz, Anna Tarnawska, Jerzy Tarnawski (1957–1965), Roman Rutkowski (reconstruction of the square: 2013)

Since the war, little has remained of the former development of the oldest market square of the city: Neumarkt, which was built in the 1530s. The majority of the historical tenements have gone, along with the meticulous Baroque fountain with a Neptune statue dating back to 1732 which was sculpted by Johann Adam Karinger to replace a medieval well. The sole remnant of the former development was Karla Löwe's City Council building from the period of World War I as well as a tenement lowered by two storeys on the northwestern corner of the square. Between 1955 and 1956, a group of the most prominent local architects developed a complex design for the new development of the square. The newly created buildings are a good example of post-war Polish Modernism and of a cohesive, consistent architectural and urban planning vision. In 2010, the Wrocław authorities announced a competition for the reconstruction of the square. The winning design was by Roman Rutkowski. The result of construction works lasting three years was an innovative public space reflecting the original Modernist development. The paving of the square consists of a regular square mesh of 5 m, made of black granite units and concrete panels. The square also features a series of structures, such as bicycle stands, dedicated benches and bench chairs, as well as planters for trees. The arrangement of the square provides multiple possibilities for organising outdoor events or setting out temporary markets. A car park is situated beneath the square which is also to include a fountain and a city pavilion in the future.

All photos: Philipp Meuser

Source: fotopolska.eu

Kozanów **109 A**

The streets Pilczycka, Gwarecka, Ignuta, Kozanowska
Miastoprojekt Wrocław
1979–1986, 1983–1992

Until the 1970s, the Kozanów district in the northwestern part of Wrocław (surrounded by green areas such as the parks of Zachodni and Pilczycki) had remained almost undeveloped. Situated within a recess, the area served as a flooding reservoir for the rivers Odra and Ślęza. Yet, due to the dynamic post-war development of the city, a design outlining the construction of a new panel estate was proposed in 1974 by the Wrocław Miastoprojekt office. Although the initial design developed by the team of architects and urban planners – supervised by Professor Tadeusz Maria Zipser – suggested moving the development further away from

Photo: Philipp Meuser

Source: fotopolska.eu

the rivers, the city proceeded with the construction of flat-roofed Modernist residential high-rises of varying height. The designers placed squares and greenery within the spaces extending between the buildings, which, combined with a looser development in comparison with traditional estates, made Kozanów a user-friendly space. Construction works were carried out in two stages between 1979 and 1986 as well as 1983 and 1992. Although a significant number of the blocks – especially those situated in closer proximity to the river – have a relatively high ground floor, this picturesque district is particularly endangered in the event of a severe flood. The flood of the century, which took place in the year 1997, brought with it the most catastrophic effects. Completely flooded, Kozanów constituted one of the most damaged parts of the city.

Photo: Philipp Meuser

Igloo House
35 Moniuszki Street
Witold Lipiński
1960–1963

110 A

This experimental house, designed and erected in the Zalesie district by the architect Witold Lipiński, is still regarded as one of the most original single-family houses to have ever been built in Poland. The Igloo House has also been permanently inhabited since. The building comprises a semi-spherical vault with a total diameter of 10 m, connected to an elliptical semi-cylindrical building housing a garage and a utility room with a glazed vestibule. On the ground floor, the interior of the copula is 75 m² and houses three small rooms distributed in the circumference, as well as a kitchen and

a central living room with a hollow in the floor. Apart from this, the building includes a mezzanine covering 35 m². An orangery was set at the back of the house. The thickness of the copula lined with aluminium foil and sheet metal is 12 cm. The structure is thermally insulated from the inside. The furniture and house furnishing elements were custom-made according to a design by Lipiński himself. The house was also equipped with an independent air heating installation that was subsequently replaced with a water installation. The Igloo House is one of the visionary designs to have been created by the architect and scientist. Among his other outstanding accomplishments are the so-called Mushroom House on Wyścigowa Street as well as the house on Szramki Street.

All photos: Filip Springer

Photo: Philipp Meuser

Przyjaźni Estate
Krzycka, Przyjaźni
Witold Molicki
1976–1980

111 A

In 1976, the Industrial Construction Company proceeded to build the Polish-Soviet Friendship Estate (Osiedle Przyjaźni) designed by Witold Molicki. The design outlined the construction of a residential complex featuring a highly original form. Its large-plate buildings with differing, gradually increasing heights – ranging from four to twelve storeys – are still one of the most interesting examples of residential housing of their time. Particular segments of the building converge at 45°, forming open circumferences which provide intimate interiors surrounded by development rings. Spacious recreational and green areas were planned among particular buildings. One of the most original elements of the estate was arguably the balcony finishing which, combined with the vibrant colours used, created an interesting and cohesive spatial composition. In 1980, a sculpture by Bogdan Hoffman, presenting a couple dancing, was placed in the estate. Today, the Przyjaźni – Friendship Estate (without the Soviet-Polish part) draws rather positive emotions, since it is probably the most tailored to fit residents' needs among the numerous large-panel estates.

1977

Source: fotopolska.eu

Photo: Philipp Meuser

2004
111 A

Photo: Stanisław Klimek

1200–1850
1850–1945
1945–1989
1990–2015

Photo: Philipp Meuser

School of English of the University of Wrocław

112 B

22 Kuźnicza Street
Maria Molicka
1992

The construction of the venue of the School of English designed by the renowned Wrocław architect Marial Molicka, the author of the Triplets – three multi-family buildings from 1968 – was completed in the year 1992. The building was erected on the corner of the streets Kuźnicza and Nożownicza on the site where the Pod Złotym Berłem tenement, which housed a hotel and a famous inn, used to stand before the war. The first design of the new building was created in 1978. In contrast to other structures intended for filling any cavities in the post-war development of the Old Town, the building is not a simple Modernist block. The three-storey tenement designed by Molicka continues the historical development of Kuźnicza Street. Vertical façade divisions create shallow roofed masonry bays. The internal yard, which is currently the office of the School of English and the Desiderius Erasmus School of Dutch, is situated on the site where the yard of the former tenements used to be, albeit covered with a glass roof. The Wrocław Enthusiasts Association awarded it the Most Elegant Building of 1992.

Photo: Philipp Meuser

Source: Solpol/Wikipedia

Solpol ↑ 113 B

21-23 Świdnicka Street
Wojciech Jarząbek, Paweł Jaszczuk, Jan Matkowski et al.
1992–1993

On 6 December 1993, an unusually modern department store, furnished with an escalator, air conditioning and monitoring, was opened on Swidnicka Street in Wrocław. Designed by Studio Ar-5, the building has remained not only the most outstanding example of Polish post-Modernism, but also one of the most controversial buildings in Wrocław. This five-storey building with a basement and a reinforced concrete frame structure occupies a corner plot. Compared with the line of development of the street, the building's front façade retracts diagonally towards the corner. The main entrance situated in the cut corner of the building was accentuated with a multi-lateral glazed tower with two bases housing the staircase. The façades of the building are covered with pink, yellow and beige ceramic tiles mounted on aluminium scaffolding. In 1999, a second department store – Solpol II – was erected opposite Solpol. Both buildings were to be connected via a glass footpath housing a café. The investor was also planning to further extend the building. These plans were, however, never realised. Due to the resignation of successive tenants, there have been rumours regarding the possible demolition of the building. Outraged, the architect and environmental specialist published a letter on this matter. As a result, an application for listing the building in the register of monuments was submitted to the Regional Monument Preserver in 2015.

Salesian Association House ↓ 114 C

2 Grunwaldzki Square
Ewa Barska, Krystyna Barska, Marian Barski
1990

In the year 1885, a neo-Gothic Church of the Heart of Jesus, which was designed by Joseph Ebers, was built upon Grunwaldzki Square. The church was adjoined by The Good Shepherd Order building complex. Over the passage of time the church buildings belonging to the Congregation were extended. Designed at the end of the 1980s by Ewa and Krystyna Barska and Marian Barski, this sacral building complex consisting of both the Salesian Association House and the extended Congregation of the Sisters of Our Lady of Mercy House continues and also lends order to the urban layout of the entire complex, with the neo-Gothic church designed by Ebers located at the centre. The masonry façade with sharp-arch windows on the one side refers to the architecture of the church while retaining a cohesive and modern expression, characteristic for the Functionalism of the 1980s by simplifying the form. A trimming and glazing of the storey located directly below the roof adds lightness and dynamism to the form.

Photo: Philipp Meuser

114 C

Photo: Philipp Meuser

Szewska Multi-functional Car Park 115 B

3a Szewska St./60 Kazimierza Wielkiego Street
Stefan Müller
2000

Photo: Masako Tomokiyo

A multi-level car park occupying nearly an entire quarter was commissioned at the beginning of 2000 in the historical Wrocław city centre. There wouldn't be anything exceptional about it if it wasn't for the fact that the building designed by Stefan Müller, built between 1998 and 1999, features a somewhat surprising form for a car park. This seven-storey flat-roofed building with rounded corners was erected on a trapezoidal floor plan and its southwestern end was accentuated with a quadrilateral tower crowned with varying-height pyramids. The last storeys were retracted by the width of a structural span. Concrete piles of varying heights created the vertical rhythm of the façade which is terminated by sheet metal triangles encircling the entire building. Since its concrete structural elements are exposed, this building acquires a distinct Brutalist character. The sharpness of its forms, such as the tower, makes reference to Expressionist forms. This car park also raises one more slightly controversial association for – it bears resemblance to numerous churches situated within the district.

Photo: Philipp Meuser

Wybrzeże Wyspiańskie Tenement
36 Wybrzeże Wyspiańskie Street
Wojciech Jarząbek
1996

116 C

In the 1990s, Wrocław experienced an outburst of creativity by the most renowned Polish post-Modernist architect, Wojciech Jarząbek, whose projects have ignited a lively debate. Following the Solpol department store built at the beginning of the 1990s, the architect designed an infill on the River Odra, awarded the Most Elegant Building of 1992 by the Wrocław Enthusiasts Association, but also deemed a "nightmare of Wybrzeże Kościuszkowskie" by architectural experts. This five-storey building with two attic levels, covered with a gable roof, draws attention with its colourful façade. A centrally positioned avant-corps with balconies, finished with a maroon balustrade, is ornamented with yellow decorations resembling lightning bolts. Although post-Modernist architecture, including its ostentatious joyful excess, has continued to stir quite a debate, mocking the prestige and aspirations of the city, it is undoubtedly a highly important certificate testifying to both the historical and architectural continuity of the city.

Photo: Philipp Meuser

Christ the King Church ↑↓ 117 A
17 Młodych Techników Street
Witold Molicki
1978–1991

The Christ the King Church located in the Szczepin district was designed by architect Witold Molicki and created at the beginning of the 1990s. The building is an example of the limitless fantasy of the creators of sacral architecture at that time.

Erected on a square floor plan, the building is crowned with four towers topped with crosses. The geometry of the diverse form of the building was emphasised by the use of various finishing materials – such as brick, roofing tile and sheet metal. The divided parts of its form add lightness, exposing the structural elements of the church. Geometrical ornaments with sharp angles were used in the bright and spacious interior of the church.

Photo: Philipp Meuser

Photo: Philipp Meuser

St. Lawrence Church ↘ 118 A
51 Odona Bujwida Street
Zenon Prętczyński, Wiktor Dziębaj
1978–1980

This post-Modernist St. Lawrence Church designed by Zenon Prętczyński, a renowned architect and co-founder of KDM, was completed in 1980. The building was erected in the location of a former nineteenth-century cemetery chapel. The building is unique, mostly due to its outstanding structure developed by the architect. The two-storey edifice rests on a monumental round reinforced concrete pile situated in the entrance zone, terminated with twelve radially distributed arms supporting the choir and therefore bearing the load of the entire form. Due to the small size of the plot, the architect designed four ledges in the form of towers or pylons on the western side to obtain maximum space. Partially glazed, the southern façade of the church is formed by dynamic arched surfaces. The entire structure is covered with a flat roof. One of the most characteristic elements of the building is its partially glazed tower, situated on the western side of the building, just next to the main entrance. The tower is crowned by a monumental cross. Today, the temple serves as an excellent example of modern architecture.

Source: iStock (Mariusz Szczygiel)

Christ the Saviour Church 119 A

2 Macedońska Street
Jadwiga Grabowska-Hawrylak, Edmund Frąckiewicz
1996–2001

In 1990, a competition was organised for a temple commemorating the Century of the Wrocław Christ the Saviour Diocese. The construction of the winning design by Jadwiga Grabowska-Hawrylak commenced in 1996. The three-aisle form of the building was erected on a rectangular floor plan and covered with a gable roof. The southern façade of the church is completed by four quadrilateral towers of varying height, with partially openwork structures added to the building later. The first of them, turned at an angle of 45°, faces the John the Baptist Archiepiscopal See, whereas the second taller one, housing a belfry, is terminated by a slim openwork spire. The building is also adjoined by four side chapels. The façade of the church is made of red brick. Works related to the interior design and furnishing of the temple, according to a design by Maristella Sienicka, were completed in the year 2007. The presbytery of the church was made of marble and the window carpentry of mahogany. To reduce the costs of construction, numerous volunteers from the parish took part in the works.

Mary, Queen of Peace Catholic Church 120 A

49 Wejherowska
Wacław Hryniewicz, Wojciech Jarząbek, Jan Matkowski
1982–1995

Settled in 1980, the competition for a design of the church on Oblatów Street was closed by selecting three Wrocław architects, one of whom was the future creator of Solpol. Perhaps this is the reason why the design of the temple is, gently speaking, very eclectic. The entire form of the building consists of two parts of differing size built on a square floor plan. These are connected with a link and a two-core tower, covered with a complex roof full of bends and elevations. The modern reinforced concrete structure of this vast two-level edifice was covered by red brick. One will clearly distinguish in both the vertical and horizontal cross-section the modified square module serving as a basis for the overall concept of the building, thanks to which the entire composition creates a complex multi-layered structure. Façade details also take on geometrical shapes. The offset church portal takes the form of a simplified Gothic arch. Richly ornamented interiors of the main storey of the church are maintained in the red palette with golden and green accents. The main aisle, separated from the ambulatory by a row of columns, is encircled by a circular aisle comprising twelve chapels. The presbytery was erected above the storey level. The basement contains education rooms and administrative offices.

All photos: Philipp Meuser

St. Ignatius of Loyola Church 121 B

16 Wincentego Stysia Street
Zenon Nasterski
1983–1986

The Institute of St. Charles Borromeo was established in 1891 on Gajowicka Street (German: Gabitzstrasse), partially renamed Wincentego Stysia Street. In the year 1929, the St. Ignatius of Loyola Church was consecrated upon this very site. Unfortunately, the entire church and the neighbouring Order of Sisters of Mercy of St. Borromeo buildings were in such a terrible technical condition that a permit for their reconstruction was obtained in 1980. The design for the entire sacral complex was developed by Zenon Nasterski. The monastic house was first built between 1980 and 1982, after which the construction of the new church commenced. The parallelogram, single-aisle temple was covered with a gable roof. From the side of Stysia Street, the western façade of the church is crowned with a characteristic tower placed above the main entrance and covered with steel sheet metal. Its shape resembles the silhouette of a pilgrim holding a cross. The vertical rhythm of this masonry façade is marked by narrow window strips. Church interiors, also designed by Nasterski, include an eighteenth-century copy of the *Salus Populi Romani*, as well as numerous stained glass elements created by Konstanty Łyskowski.

Church of the Holy Spirit

122 A

2-4 Bardzka Street
Tadeusz Zipser, Waldemar Wawrzyniak, Jerzy Wojnarowicz
1973–1994

Since the 1950s, efforts have been made to rebuild the Church of the Holy Spirit, created in 1929 and destroyed during the war. It was only in 1971 that the then authorities permitted the construction of a church on the site. The end result was an original edifice inspired by organic architecture. This two-storey building with a tight form was erected on a quasi-hexagonal floor plan and has a reinforced concrete frame. The entire structure was covered with a steel-framed roof which resembles a cone and is crowned with a cross. The tower-like roof was covered with copper sheet metal and the façades of the building were made of raw brick. The western façade consisting of seven ogive windows includes the main entrance preceded by two-wing stairs. The interior of the church, capable of accommodating nearly 2,000 people, is decorated, among other things, with paintings by Tadeusz Zipser and a grand Christ statue sculpted by Jerzy Romasz. Unfortunately, as a result of thermal insulation works performed several years ago without any consultation with the architects, the building was painted orange and furnished with cheap-looking plastic windows located above the entrance.

All photos: Philipp Meuser

Photo: Philipp Meuser

St. Stanislaus Kostka Church 123 A

91 Hubska Street
Stefan Müller, Maria Müller, Barbara Jaworska
1986–2006

Before the war, this site housed a small masonry evangelical chapel. The year 1984 marked the beginning of construction of one of the most original examples of contemporary sacral architecture in Poland. The main designer of the edifice, the renowned architect Stefan Müller, opposed the treatment of churches as "sculptural" subjects. He was an advocate of modern architecture – also in the sacral realm. The St. Stanislaus Kostka Church is an excellent example of such an approach to architecture. In contrast to numerous kitschy historicising buildings created at that time, the temple situated in the Huby estate draws attention with its simplicity and consistence of vision. The modern basilica three-aisle church with a reinforced concrete structure is covered with a flat roof. Although the façade is made entirely out of brick of various shades, it is arranged in such a manner so as to create distinct square fields. The monumental façade with the main entrance, topped with a large rectangular window, is flanked by two giant pylons of varying height. With its stone floor and narrow rectangular windows, the interior of the church is maintained as minimal as possible. A simple and massive belfry is located to the north of the church.

Photo: Philipp Meuser

Photo: dar_wro

Hotel Mercure Panorama ↓

124 B

1 Dominikański Square
Studio EL - Edward Lach, Anna Rumińska, Jan Mytkowski
1999–2000

A multi-functional facility housing both a hotel and a shopping centre was built in the place of the former Panorama hotel in 2000. Its spatial layout reflects the former street arrangement, whereas its architecture refers to the historical space of Dominikański Square. This six-storey building with a basement, featuring a reinforced concrete slab-pile structure with stiffening walls, was erected on a multi-lateral floor plan and covered with a flat roof. The dark brown façades of the building, referring to the Gothic architecture of the neighbourhood, are made of clinker brick. The geometrical façade composition is formed by a grid of square windows. A rectangular glazing is placed above the main entrance and reaches the roof line. The side wall of the hotel building, consisting of glass panel segments, provides a reflection of the Gothic St. Adalbert Church. The design also put forward the renovation of the vicinity of the building. The diverse texture of the square and sidewalk paving from the side of Czesława Streets reflects the outline of the former city fortifications.

New Airport Terminal ↑

125 A

Graniczna Street
JSK Architekci
2009–2011

The new passenger terminal of the Wrocław International Airport was commissioned on 11 March 2012. Designed by JSK Architekci and built by Hochtief Polska, the building is one of the largest structures of this type in Poland. Located to the west of the remaining development, the terminal housing both the functions related to the airport apron and those related to the city services was created as a single-space hall with a completely glazed façade. With three above-ground storeys and one underground storey, this rectangular building was covered with a dynamic, wavy and also partially glazed roof. The roof structure was divided into 15 m segments. A system of slim diagonal V-shaped columns supporting the roof structure lend order to the building's spacious and perfectly illuminated interior with a light shimmering floor. Using dedicated cantilevers, the girders supporting the roof have been installed outside the outline of the building, both on the side of the access road and that of the airport apron. The terminal has two main entrances – that to the north and that to the east.

Photo: Philipp Meuser

Source: iStock (Mariusz Szczygiel)

Regional Business Tourism Centre

126 C

1 Wystawowa Street
ch+ architekci, VROA architekci
2009–2010

An international architectural competition for the design of the restaurant pavilion of the Regional Business Tourism Centre, located next to the Centennial Hall, was settled in 2007. The winning design by ch+ architekci and VROA architekci proposed the renovation and extension of this historical pavilion building. In the course of renovation, part of the pergola dismantled after the war was restored and the external terraces were recreated. Window carpentry was also replaced in the historical pavilion and the representative central lobby was renovated. The most important element of the design was the extension of the pavilion by two rooms and a restaurant. The new functions were allocated to two historical pavilions flanking the historical building. In turn, building service rooms were placed in the underground of the existing pavilion. All of the steel-frame buildings feature entirely glazed three-part façades. The eastern wing houses a large auditorium, whereas the western wing contains a multi-functional room. The minimalist interiors built on a symmetrical floor plan are dominated by white, grey and graphite. A restaurant was located along the façade of the historical pavilion, from the side of the pergola.

Photo: Philipp Meuser

Capitol Music Theatre ↓

127 B

67 Piłsudskiego Street
KKM Kozień Architekci
2013

The extension of the historical auditorium of the former Capitol cinema-theatre was completed in 2013 according to a design by KKM Kozień Architekci. Apart from the historical heritage of the building and the current development of the Kościuszko residential estate, the building also reflected the space of the city square located at the junction of the streets Piłsudskiego and Świdnicka, created as a result of post-war changes in the development of this area. For this very reason, the northwestern corner of the flat-roofed building, with a massive geometrical form and smooth stone façade glazed in several places, was particularly accentuated. A transitional zone between the space of the square and the interior of the building was created. The main entrance, accessed from the two streets Swidnicka and Piłsudskiego, leads to a glass-roof lobby located in the place of the former internal yard, which leads to the foyer housing the cloakrooms, and to the ground floor of the auditorium. From the side of Piłsudskiego Street, the building houses a ticket box and a corridor leading to the underground chamber music stage and a restaurant. The renovation project also proposed the renovation of the stage complex and the Modernist Odra Film film institution building.

← Centre of Applied Arts (Academy of Fine Arts in Wrocław)

128 B

19-21 Romualda Traugutta Street
Pracownia Architektury Głowacki
2012

The new building of the Academy of Fine Arts was erected on the corner of the streets Traugutta and Krasińskiego. The cost of the investment was more than 53 million *zlotys*. The end result was an eight-storey (seven above ground and one underground) functional building with a tight geometric form, not only matching the frontage of the neighbouring streets, but also lending order to the chaotic development of this part of the city. The entirely glass façade, adding lightness to the building, contains modernly decorated interiors housing, among other things, design studios, a ceramics workshop, an auditorium for 150 people, film and photography laboratories and even a mini-mill for melting glass. A car park and warehouses were located below the ground level. The most important element of the entire complex was the garden of the Academy of Fine Arts, situated from the side of Traugutta Street. This way, this monolithic building constitutes a green oasis in the busy city centre.

Photo: Philipp Meuser

Africanarium and Oceanarium at Wrocław ZOO

129 C

1-5 Wróblewskiego Street
ARC2 Fabryka Projektowa
2012–2014

One of the most interesting and boldest architectural visions completed in Wrocław in recent years, this Africanarium and Oceanarium building at Wrocław ZOO, finished in 2014, is situated in the vicinity of the Centennial Hall. Erected on a rectangular floor plan with a diagonal of 160 m and covered with a flat roof, this reinforced concrete building is covered with black Corian façades, resting on a steel frame. A shallow, rectangular swimming pool which reflects the wavy façade is located in front of the rounded, northern façade of the building. The interior of the building accommodates a central multi-functional space with five satellite African biotope rooms and a view terrace. A water tank with animal ranges, accessible from both inside and outside the building, is situated in its southern part. Unfortunately, the interior and exhibition design do not reflect the aesthetically refined architecture of the building.

All photos: Philipp Meuser

Source: iStock (Gosiek-B)

Sky Tower 130 A
95 Powstańców Śląskich Street
Studio Architektoniczne Fold
2007–2012

With a height of 206 m, Poland's tallest residential and office building was completed in 2012. Erected in the city centre and enclosed by the streets Śląskich, Wielka, Powstańców Gwiaździsta and Szczęśliwa, this high-rise belonging to LC Corp Sky was built in the place of the Poltegor – a dismantled high-rise dating back to the 1980s. Within the course of the construction process, the architectural concept behind the building was changed several times. The first design, selected in the 2006 competition, was developed by the Warsaw-based studio named B&G. However, the final form of the building is the result of the concept proposed by the Fold studio. The entire residential, office and commercial complex was to comprise six segments. However, only three of these were ultimately completed. The complex comprises a four-storey "base" building erected upon a square floor plan with rounded corners housing, among other things, a shopping centre and a nineteen-storey "sail" adjoining the tower, built on the floor plan of a slightly bent arch. The glass façade of the building has a clear horizontal rhythm, thanks to the visible storey divisions. The building has raised some controversies, not only due to its questionable architecture, but, most of all, due to its dominating role in this part of the city, or even the entire city.

Wrocław City Stadium
1 Śląska Alley
JSK Architekci
2009–2011

131 A

In the year 2007, the Wrocław authorities announced a competition for the design of the City Stadium. The winning concept of a Chinese lantern, reflecting Modernist architectural traditions, was created by JSK Architekci. The most outstanding element of the stadium is its bright façade made of semi-transparent fibreglass mesh covered with Teflon, thanks to which the form of this giant, nearly 40 m tall stadium achieves lightness and an innovative minimalist character. The stadium was built on a wide platform of nearly 53 m^2, leading to the stadium from the two streets Lotnicza and Królewiecka. Another interesting feature, with regard to the style of the stadium, are holes of varying size where trees were planted. Both a car park and technical rooms were organised beneath the platform. The next four-storey parking lot was designed next to the stadium. The facility was furnished with one-level auditoriums accommodating more than 45,000 visitors. The City Stadium was one of the investments created for the purpose of the 2012 UEFA European Championship.

Source: iStock (Mariusz Szczygiel)

Source: iStock (PM78)

New University of Wrocław Library ↑ 132 B

13 Fryderyka Joliot-Curie Street
Jacek Rzyski, Jerzy Ruszkowski, Jacek Kopczewski
2003–2012

This investment worth nearly a quarter of a million by the University of Wrocław experienced a series of misfortunes. The architectural competition for the library building in a quarter between the streets Wyszyńskiego and Szczytnicka was announced and settled in 1999, but the construction process was only completed in 2011 after numerous contractor changes. Ultimately, the building was officially opened a year later. Situated by the River Odra, near the Pokoju Bridge, the building consists of two tight forms separated by a pedestrian passageway. The massive flat-roofed geometric building featuring a reinforced concrete structure bears clear reference to monumental Modernist architecture. From the side of the river, the façade includes a characteristic element in the form of massive pillars overlooking the boulevards. The simple form, nearly devoid of details, is covered with a light-grey façade made of stone cladding. Initially, the façade was to be covered by limestone, but the raw material ultimately used was sandstone. The spacious but raw interiors of the building are also dominated by raw concrete and stone.

Faculty of Law, Administration and Economics of the University of Wrocław ↓ 133 B

7-10 Uniwersytecka Street
Maćków Pracownia Projektowa
2001–2003

The competition for the new office of the Faculty of Law of the University of Wrocław, located within the Old Town, was settled in 1999. The winning concept by Pracownia Projektowa Maćków, proposing the construction of an edifice reflecting the scale and form of development present in the area, bore clear resemblance to the Modernist architecture of Wrocław. Erected at the junction of Kuźnicza Street and Uniwersytecki Square, the building consisted of two wings. The main entrance, the two-storey representative lobby and a restaurant were situated on the side facing Kuźnicza Street. Didactic rooms and a library were placed on higher levels.

Photo: Philipp Meuser

Photo: Philipp Meuser

Two large auditoriums, one placed on top of another, were situated in the rounded, totally glazed corner, exposing the internal structure of the building. The geometric form of the building is covered by a simple detail-free façade made of travertine cladding, with irregularly distributed rectangular windows featuring dark carpentry. Modernly furnished interiors were finished with glass, stone and natural wood. The glass façade from the side of Uniwersytecki Square reflects the Baroque University Church.

Integrated Transfer Node ↑↓ 134 A

Maślice
Maćków Pracownia Projektowa
2010–2011

Resembling a kite, the integrated transfer node designed by the Maćków design office was nominated for the 2013 European Mies van der Rohe Award. Connecting a railway stop situated at ground level with a fast city tram stop situated upon a platform consisting of two viaducts, the transfer node can direct pedestrian

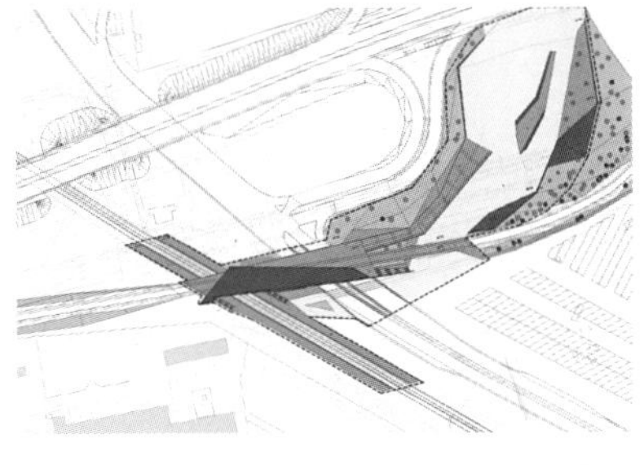

traffic to the City Stadium. The designers placed a triangular reinforced concrete roof on to the platform adapted to dense human traffic. Furthermore, a wide ramp with a gentle slop in the direction of the stadium platform was installed. The two levels were connected by stairs and two elevators for the handicapped. The dynamic form of the simple and functional roof of the building – made entirely out of raw architectural concrete with elements of zinced steel, reflecting the features of Deconstructivist architecture – not only gives the structure a modern touch, but also reflects the context of its space, dominated by the multi-level road junction of the Wrocław ring road.

Source: iStock (oleksajewicz)

Photo: Philipp Meuser

Silver Tower Centre 135 B
Konstytucji 3 Maja Square
Maćków Pracownia Projektowa
2014

Built in the Wrocław city centre, right next to the main railway station on the site of the former bus station, this multi-functional structure consists of two main geometric forms with mutually shifted edges resembling displaced boxes. The lower six-storey segment houses a hotel. The taller fourteen-storey segment, constructed out of blocks of differing size, includes offices which can be randomly shaped thanks to the innovative, reinforced concrete structure. The rhythm of the glass façade of the building is marked by vertical profiles resulting from functional requirements. This simple and modern building with a dynamic form is perfectly incorporated into the local urban fabric. A restored advertisement post from the 1930s was placed in front of the building.

Source: iStock (Jan Hetman)

Photo: Bartek Barczyk

Green Day
9 Szczytnicka Street
Maćków Pracownia Projektowa
2014

136 B

Situated in the downtown, this green office building designed by Pracownia Projektowa Maćków includes eight storeys – six above ground and two underground levels. The innovative flat-roofed building features a reinforced concrete structure, a U-shaped floor plan and an internal yard separating two wings and housing a recreational space. The main entrance to the building in the form of an arcade, decorated with an aluminium mosaic, is situated on the corner of the façade from the side of Szczytnicka Street. The geometric form of this light-grey façade is marked with a regular grid of windows, slightly retracted in reference to the face of the building. Simple timeless building divisions were emphasised by the use of dark window carpentry.

Source: iStock (Max Topchij)

Thespian ↑ 137 A

1-3 Powstańców Śląskich Square
Maćków Pracownia Projektowa
2009–2011

The architecture of this building refers to the character of the low historical development of Powstańców Śląskich Square on the one hand, while reflecting the high development of Powstańców Śląskich Street on the other – hence the form of the building completing the development of the square and its vicinity is clearly divided into a lower two-storey base housing services and offices and the taller three-wing residential part. The eastern wing of the building is topped with a tower, while the rear part includes an internal yard. The double glass façade with shutters installed in aluminium metalwork is formed by large panels contained by concrete cornices and divided by vertical wooden elements. The designers were able to create a modern and elegant form corresponding to the development of Powstańców Square. The building has two entrances. The main entrance leads to the commercial part and is situated in the corner arcade of the pedestal from the side of Powstańców Street.

Szymanowski School of Music 138 B

25 Piłsudskiego Street
Maćków Pracownia Projektowa
2010–2014

Established in 1946, the School of Music received a new venue on the representative Józefa Piłsudskiego Street in 2014. The building, which merged perfectly with the frontage of the street, neighbours with the Wrocław Philharmonic. Its simple massive form was erected on a square floor plan and comprises four segments enclosing an internal yard. The structure adjoining Piłsudskiego Street and the two side wings house didactic functions – namely practice and music rooms. To the south, the yard is enclosed by a chamber music hall. Gyms were situated in the underground parts beneath the concert hall. The five-storey flat-roofed building also houses two recording studios with improved acoustics, a caféteria and a sports court. The form of the building was cleared of any redundant details. The smooth bright façade includes irregularly distributed, gradually reduced windows. The diverse window configuration adds a three-dimensional character to the façade. The modern minimalist interiors were finished with raw architectural concrete.

Wrocław University of Technology Campus

139 C

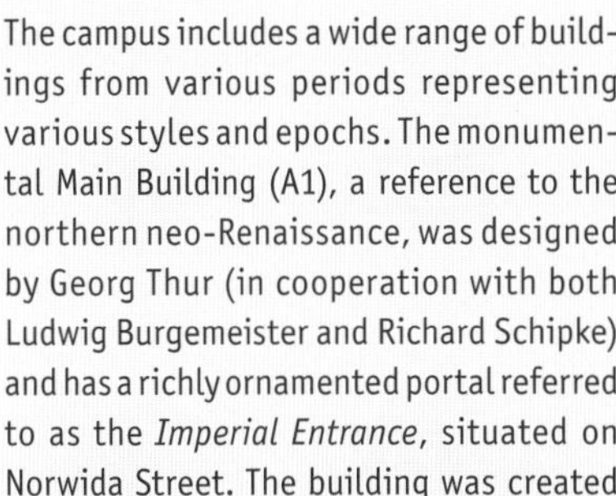

Grunwaldzki Square, the streets Marii Skłodowskiej-Curie and Wybrzeże Wyspiańskiego
Georg Thur, Ludwig Burgemeister
1910, 1925

The campus includes a wide range of buildings from various periods representing various styles and epochs. The monumental Main Building (A1), a reference to the northern neo-Renaissance, was designed by Georg Thur (in cooperation with both Ludwig Burgemeister and Richard Schipke) and has a richly ornamented portal referred to as the *Imperial Entrance*, situated on Norwida Street. The building was created in two stages between 1910 and 1925. The Modernist Faculty of Land and Marine Civil Engineering (C7), completed in 1981, stands out the most among the group of post-war buildings. Although neglected, the building still impresses with its innovative form featuring truncated corners and with its original blue glass façade which may be soon destroyed by thermal insulation. Another example of a positive renovation of a Socialist Modernist building is the edifice designed by Andrzej Frydecki, completed in 1953. The most interesting of all of the contemporary buildings in the complex is surely the Integrated Student Centre of the Wrocław University of Technology, marked with the symbol C-13.

All photos: Philipp Meuser

Integrated Student Centre of the Wrocław University of Technology (C-13) ↑ 140 C

23 Wybrzeże Wyspiańskiego St.
Manufaktura Nr 1
2007

Situated in the campus of the Wrocław University of Technology, the Student Centre building was created to integrate students attending the first year of their studies. To the south, the building closes up the main axis of the campus. The form of the building consists of two wings: the larger front wing situated along the course of Wybrzeże Wyspiańskiego Street, including office spaces, is crossed by the lower side wing housing auditoriums and a buffet. These are connected by a large two-storey common space with a café. The façade is an important element of the building. The concrete façades are covered with smooth chipboard-cement panel modules containing one or two round window holes which create a unique composition of unevenly perforated panels to reflect the first computers. The random façade arrangement also creates an exceptional climate inside the building.

Wrocław University of Technology Library ↓ 141 C

11 Grunwaldzki Square
Heinle, Wischer und Partner Architekci
2013

A competition for the Wrocław University of Technology Library, incorporated into the urban space of the school's campus, was carried out in 2007. The winning design proposed by Heinle, Wischer und Partner outlined the construction of a building enclosing Grunwaldzki Square. Topped with a flat partially glazed roof, this four-storey building consisting of several straight forms devoid of any details (with an extensive central part situated on the ground floor) became a gate to the campus. Its light façade with a delicate horizontal division and irregularly distributed large geometrical glazing panels added an elegant and modern touch to the building. Its well-lit minimalist interiors accommodating more than half a thousand people were finished with wood. What is immediately notable about the interior is the open staircase leading to successive levels of the building.

GEOCENTRUM ↑

142 C

13/15 Na Grobli Street
Kuryłowicz & Associates
2010–2012

This new Faculty of Geoengineering, Mining and Geology, Marine and Land Civil Engineering and Mechanics and Power Engineering of the Wrocław University of Technology was completed in 2012. The new venue constitutes stage one of a larger investment implemented by the UoT on the left bank of River Odra. This five-storey building consists of three longitudinal forms located on a shared one-floor platform running on the north-south axis. Internal yards providing even illumination of all segments are situated between particular complex parts. The entire structure refers to Modernist architecture. The southern façade overlooking the river, covered with white plaster, is horizontally divided by long strips of windows in black metalwork. The remaining façades have been covered with black clinker brock and completed with an irregular layout of narrow vertical windows and large geometric longitudinal glazing. Apart from the window arrangement and façade variation, the rhythmic layout of particular buildings is dynamised by a slightly inclined roof resulting from the changing height of the vertical forms: four storeys to the south and five to the north.

Sports and Recreation Hall ↓

143 B

29-31 Ks. Piotra Skargi Street
Major Architekci
2010

An architectural competition for the sports hall within High School Complex No. 2 was settled in 2007. The biggest challenge for the designers of the building was its very location. The hall was placed between two buildings from the turn of the nineteenth and twentieth centuries: the school complex designed by Richard Plüddemann and Karl Klimm and the tenement housing the Visual Arts High School. This specific context and its dominating function were the determining factors in the formation of the design. Major Architekci created a building comprising several simple forms covered with flat roofs, housing not only a sports hall, but also sports courts, a gym and a climbing hall. A large lobby links the hall to the school building. One of the most characteristic elements of the building is the openwork screen situated between the buildings from the side of Nowa Street, intended to mask the chaotic cubature of the forms with varying height. Made of perforated CORTEN, the screen not only adjusts the illumination of the rooms, but also creates a homogenous frontage merging with the neighbouring development. Raw industrial interiors are an extension of the external form of the building.

All photos: Philipp Meuser

The Granary Hotel ↑↓ 144 B
24 Mennicza Street
Gottesman Szmelcman Architecture
2005

Located within a reconstructed sixteenth-century granary, this luxurious hotel was designed by the Parisian Gottesman Szmelcman Architecture company. Erected in the year 1565, the granary was part of the nearby brewery as of 1796 and produced malt. The masonry form of the building, of which only the basements, the peripheral walls and the apexes have been preserved, is covered with a gable glass roof. Its steel structure imitates the original division of the building into three storeys. The above-ground part houses minimalist and elegantly furnished guestsrooms and apartments. In turn, the reception desk, restaurants, fitness and spa rooms are situated in the former basements. Their stylish interiors are decorated by raw non-plastered brick. The highest attic levels contain a conference room and the largest two-floor apartments. A small green yard can be found at the back of the plot. Completed in 2005, the building houses a total of forty-seven apartments but does not provide any parking spaces.

Corte Verona ↗→ 145 A
2 Pracy Alley
Biuro Projektów Lewicki Łatak
2010

Erected on a quadrilateral floor plan with an internal yard and a flat roof, this building of varying heights, designed by the Krakow-based Lewicki and Łatak office, is situated in the vicinity of the estate designed by Paul Heim and Albert Kempter near Grabiszyński Park. The form of the building refers to the structure of a masonry wall. Its characteristic façades, shaped by protruding loggias, create a geometrical spatial layout. From the side

of Pracy Alley, the façade of the building continues this pattern in a slightly more ordered manner, maintaining the development line which is established by the neighbouring buildings. The façade made of clinker brick was finished with natural-coloured wooden window carpentry and ceramic elements. Despite this diversified form, the simple shapes create a typical enclosed space of a fenced estate.

All photos: Philipp Meuser

Photo: Thomas Michael Krüger

Marina 146 B

2 Księcia Witolda Street

Artur Wójciak

2006–2012

Topacz Development commenced the construction of the Marina on Księcia Witolda Street on the Kępa Mieszczańska island in 2006. It is a complex of two buildings intended for commercial and residential purposes. In 2009, the first of these was commissioned – the one designed by Studio Wójciak Jagodziński incorporated into the Archipelag Group. A marina for sail boats was situated next to the building. This four-storey building with an underground parking lot was covered with a gable roof without eaves. Its simple form was extended by crosswise wings covered with flat roofs. The clinker façade of the building is completed by large geometric glazing and wooden finishing elements. The year 2012 marked the completion of the Marina II three-storey building comprising several simple forms with a retracted ground floor and a flat roof. Its horizontally divided façade is formed by external vertical shutters made of light wood. From the portside, its clinker façade is divided by regularly distributed loggias supplemented by bays situated in the corners. The investor has already announced the construction of the third building.

Source: iStock (kelifamily)

Photo: Philipp Meuser

PWST ↑↗ 147 A

59 Braniborska Street
Bogna Klimczewska (1969–1972), KKM Kozień Architekci (extension: 2011)

Completed in 2011, the extension of the Wrocław division of the State Higher School of Filmmaking was designed by the Krakow-based KKM Kozień Architekci office. A Modernist building housing the former Construction Worker Culture Centre designed by Bogna Klimczewska was adapted for the purposes of the school. In order to implement all design proposals, the designers created a new spatial arrangement which enters into a dialogue with the old development. A complex of several rounded buildings housing didactic rooms, spatially tied to the existing series of administrative rooms and the stage tower superstructure, was built in the east. One of the most characteristic elements of the building is the use of copper plates on the extended structures. What is noteworthy is the rounded golden metal-plated two-storey structure adjoining the main entrance. The central part of the complex is the two-storey lobby illuminated by a grand window. The new part housing rehearsal rooms, locker rooms, lecture halls and recording studios is situated at its circumference. The old but upgraded building contains the second zone featuring, among other things, theatre stages with a shared foyer, a ticket box, a buffet and a guest cloakroom.

House on Water ↓ 148 B

5a Wybrzeże Słowackiego Street
Kamil Zaremba
2005–2013

Poland's first house on water was completed in 2013 in Wrocław. In Kamil Zaremba's house, foundations are replaced with concrete (not plastic) floats. To obtain the lightest form possible, the walls of the building were made of prefabricated Styrofoam panels resting on a metal frame. The grey façade of this flat-roofed building erected upon a rectangular floor plan is dynamised by colourful geometrical fragments: irregularly distributed glazing. The building is heated by an electrical installation and an air pump. This year-round, fully furnished house has a total footprint of 250 m^2. Initially, the house was to include two storeys, but it was proven that only a one-floor structure would be able to float under the majority of Wrocław bridges.

Photo: Bartek Barczyk

Rędziński Bridge

Zespół Badawczo-Projektowy Mosty-Wrocław

2011

149 A

This cable-stayed bridge on the River Odra and the Rędzińska Isle is part of the highway ring road of the city. The passage is situated near the Rędzin sluice. The Rędziński Bridge is not only the longest suspended ceiling in Poland – with a total length measuring 512 m – but also the largest reinforced concrete bridge across the world. The reinforced concrete structure of the bridge is suspended by 160 cables on one of the tallest pylons in Poland of 122 m. The overall cost of this 30 tonne bridge, designed by a research and design team supervised by Professor Jan Biliszczuk, was 576 million *zlotys*. The contractor for the project was Mostostal Warszawa and Acciona Infraestructuras.

Source: iStock (FikMik)

National Forum of Music 150 B
Wolności Square
APA Kuryłowicz
2010–2015

An international competition for the new venue of the National Forum of Music and its vicinity was settled in 2005. In 2015, the construction of this multi-functional building designed by APA Kuryłowicz was completed. The building was erected in the city centre, surrounded by the historical development of Wolności Square. This nine-storey (six above ground and three underground) building houses a main auditorium for 1,800 guests, three chamber music rooms, a recording studio as well as the necessary amenities. The form of the building was subjected to its functions – hence the requirement to obtain the best acoustic properties possible. Therefore, the vault of the

Photo: Lukasz Rajchert

Photo: Thomas Michael Krüger

main auditorium is covered with a special acoustic ceiling made of moveable gypsum prefabricated elements. Its lateral walls include special resonance chambers used to control the acoustic makeup of the interior. The building's interior design by Towarzystwo Projektowe is devoid of any leitmotif. Randomly selected finishing materials, combined with an unfortunate spatial arrangement, create a bland whole. The façade of the massive building was covered with dark wooden composite panels and golden aluminium. Its horizontal rhythm is emphasised by narrow strips of horizontal glazing. The front façade draws attention with its large rectangular window located just above the main entrance. The spatial development around the building is undoubtedly one of its weakest points. The spacious square does in no way encourage one to spend their quality time inside.

Photo: Lukasz Rajchert

A
PRACZE ODRZAŃSKIE
Oder
A8
149
Autostrada Obwodnica Wrocławia (AOW)
MAŚLICE
336
LEŚNICA
026
Kosmonautów
94
131
PILCZYCE
109
KOZANÓW
Pilczycka
134
Lotnicza
120
FABRYCZNA
GADÓW
KUŹNIKI
POPOWIC
5
ŻERNIKI
A8
NOWY DWÓR
125
Copernicus Airport Wrocław
MUCHOBÓR MAŁY
Autostrada Obwodnica Wrocławia (AOW)
Klecińska
104
MUCHOBÓR WIELKI
145
GRABISZY
GRABISZYNE
OPORÓW
KLECINA
3 km
http://goo.gl/RhPvsR
A5

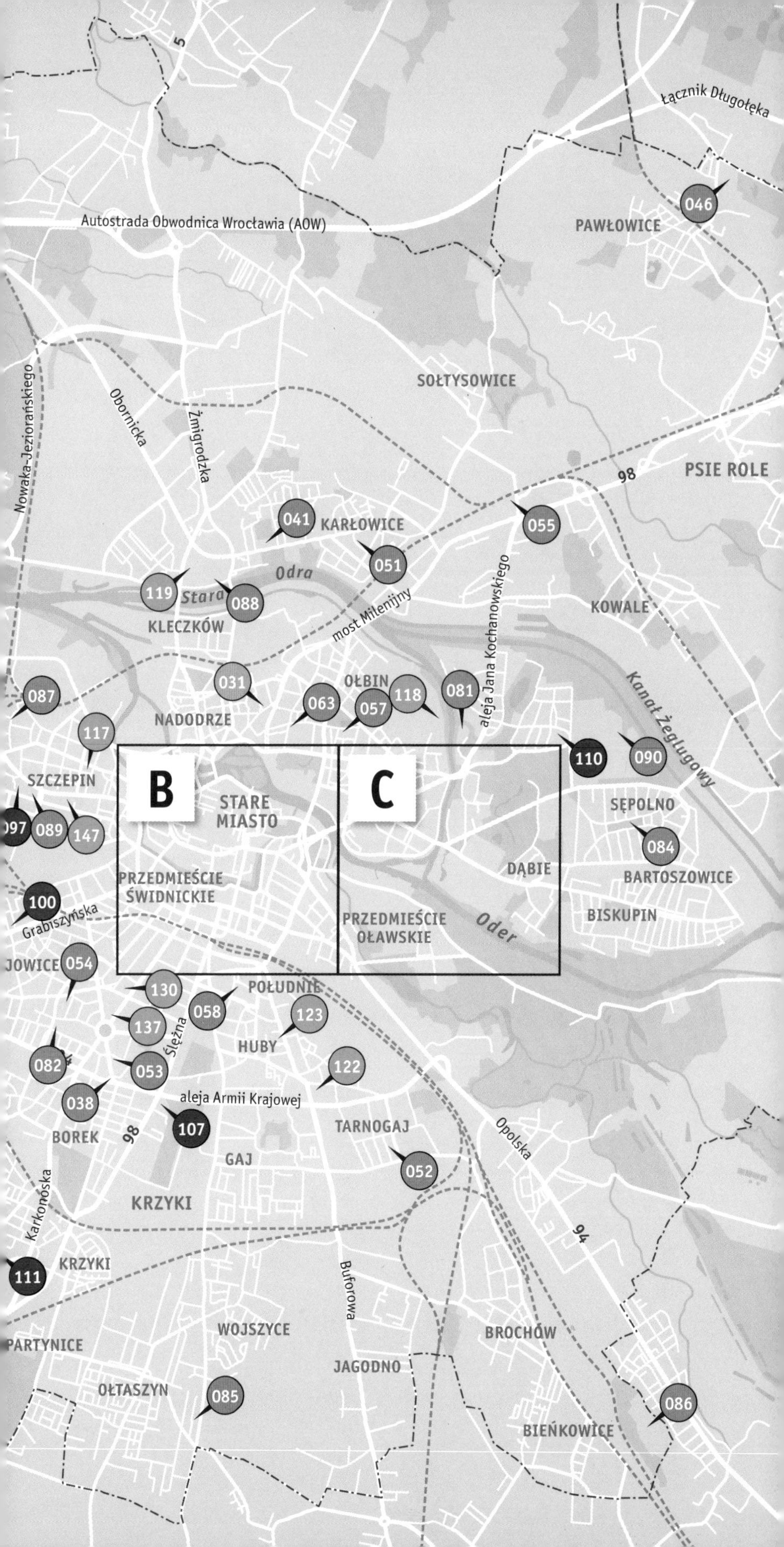

Łącznik Długołęka
Autostrada Obwodnica Wrocławia (AOW)
PAWŁOWICE
SOŁTYSOWICE
PSIE ROLE
Obornicka
Żmigrodzka
Nowaka-Jeziorańskiego
KARŁOWICE
Odra
Stara
KLECZKÓW
most Milenijny
aleja Jana Kochanowskiego
KOWALE
Kanał Żeglugowy
NADODRZE
OŁBIN
SZCZEPIN
B
C
STARE MIASTO
SĘPOLNO
PRZEDMIEŚCIE ŚWIDNICKIE
DĄBIE
BARTOSZOWICE
Grabiszyńska
PRZEDMIEŚCIE OŁAWSKIE
Oder
BISKUPIN
POŁUDNIE
HUBY
Ślężna
aleja Armii Krajowej
TARNOGAJ
BOREK
GAJ
KRZYKI
Opolska
Karkonoska
KRZYKI
Buforowa
WOJSZYCE
BROCHÓW
PARTYNICE
JAGODNO
OŁTASZYN
BIEŃKOWICE

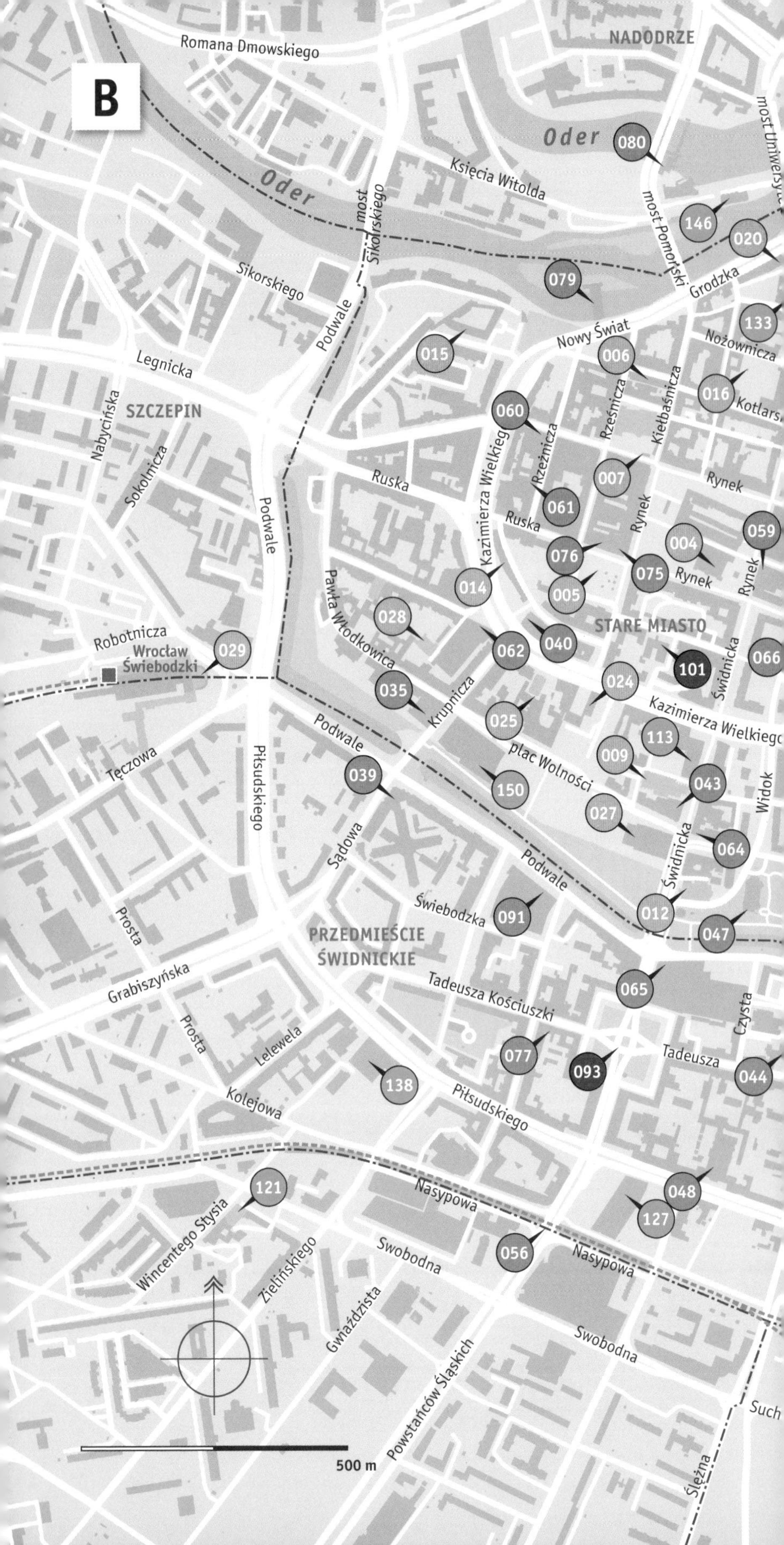
B
Romana Dmowskiego
NADODRZE
Oder
Oder
Księcia Witolda
most Sikorskiego
most Pomorski
most Uniwersytecki
Sikorskiego
Podwale
Grodzka
Nowy Świat
Nożownicza
Legnicka
Kotlarska
SZCZEPIN
Nabycińska
Sokolnicza
Ruska
Kazimierza Wielkiego
Rzeźnicza
Rześnicza
Kiełbaśnicza
Rynek
Podwale
Ruska
Rynek
Rynek
Rynek
Pawła Włodkowica
STARE MIASTO
Robotnicza
Wrocław Świebodzki
Krupnicza
Świdnicka
Kazimierza Wielkiego
Podwale
Tęczowa
Piłsudskiego
plac Wolności
Widok
Sądowa
Świdnicka
Podwale
Świebodzka
Prosta
PRZEDMIEŚCIE ŚWIDNICKIE
Tadeusza Kościuszki
Grabiszyńska
Czysta
Prosta
Lelewela
Tadeusza
Kolejowa
Piłsudskiego
Nasypowa
Wincentego Stysia
Zielińskiego
Swobodna
Nasypowa
Gwiaździsta
Swobodna
Powstańców Śląskich
Sucha
500 m
Ślężna
080
146
020
079
133
015
006
016
060
007
061
059
004
076
075
014
005
028
040
062
029
101
066
035
024
025
113
009
039
150
043
027
064
012
091
047
065
077
093
044
138
121
048
127
056

Wyspa Bielarska
Wyspa Słodowa
Wyspa Młyńska
Tamka
Wyspa Piasek
Ogród Botaniczny
plac Katedralny
Kardynała Stefana Wyszyńskiego
Szczytnicka
Szewska
Grodzka
Kuźnicza
plac Nankiera
Oder
Piaskowa
most Pokoju
Kotlarska
Jana Ewangelisty Purkyniego
Park Juliusza Słowackiego
Krawiecka
plac Powstańców Warszawy
Oławska
Mazowiecka
Generała Romualda Traugutta
Wierzbowa
Mennicza
Księdza Piotra Skargi
Nowa
Teatralna
Wzgórze Partyzantów
Podwale
Zygmunta Krasińskiego
Stanisława Worcella
Komuny Paryskiej
Generała Kazimierza Pułaskiego
Kościuszki
Tadeusza Kościuszki
Dąbrowskiego
Hugona Kołłątaja
Dworcowa
Piłsudskiego
Wrocław Główny
Sucha
002
003
011
001
008
022
023
021
069
136
106
132
112
018
019
108
098
095
045
010
033
017
092
036
124
078
068
148
067
115
143
144
128
049
032
105
050
103
096
135
034
030

C
OŁBIN
Henryka Sienkiewicza
Nowowiejska
Piastowska
Grunwaldzka
Grunwaldzka
099
102
plac Grunwaldzki
PLAC GRUNWALDZKI
083
Szczytnicka
094
plac Grunwaldzki
plac Grunwaldzki
139
114
Norwida
Tytusa Chałubińskiego
042
wybrzeże Ludwika Pasteura
Marii Skłodowskiej-Curie
141
Kamila
Cypriana
Mariana Smoluchowskiego
Łukasiewicza
Ignacego
116
most Zwierzyniecki
140
wybrzeże Stanisława Wyspiańskiego
Wyspa Szczytnicka
Stara Odra
142
037
Na Grobli
PRZEDMIEŚCIE OŁAWSKIE
Międzyrzecka
Rakowiecka
Okólna
Na Niskich Łąkach
Tadeusza Kościuszki

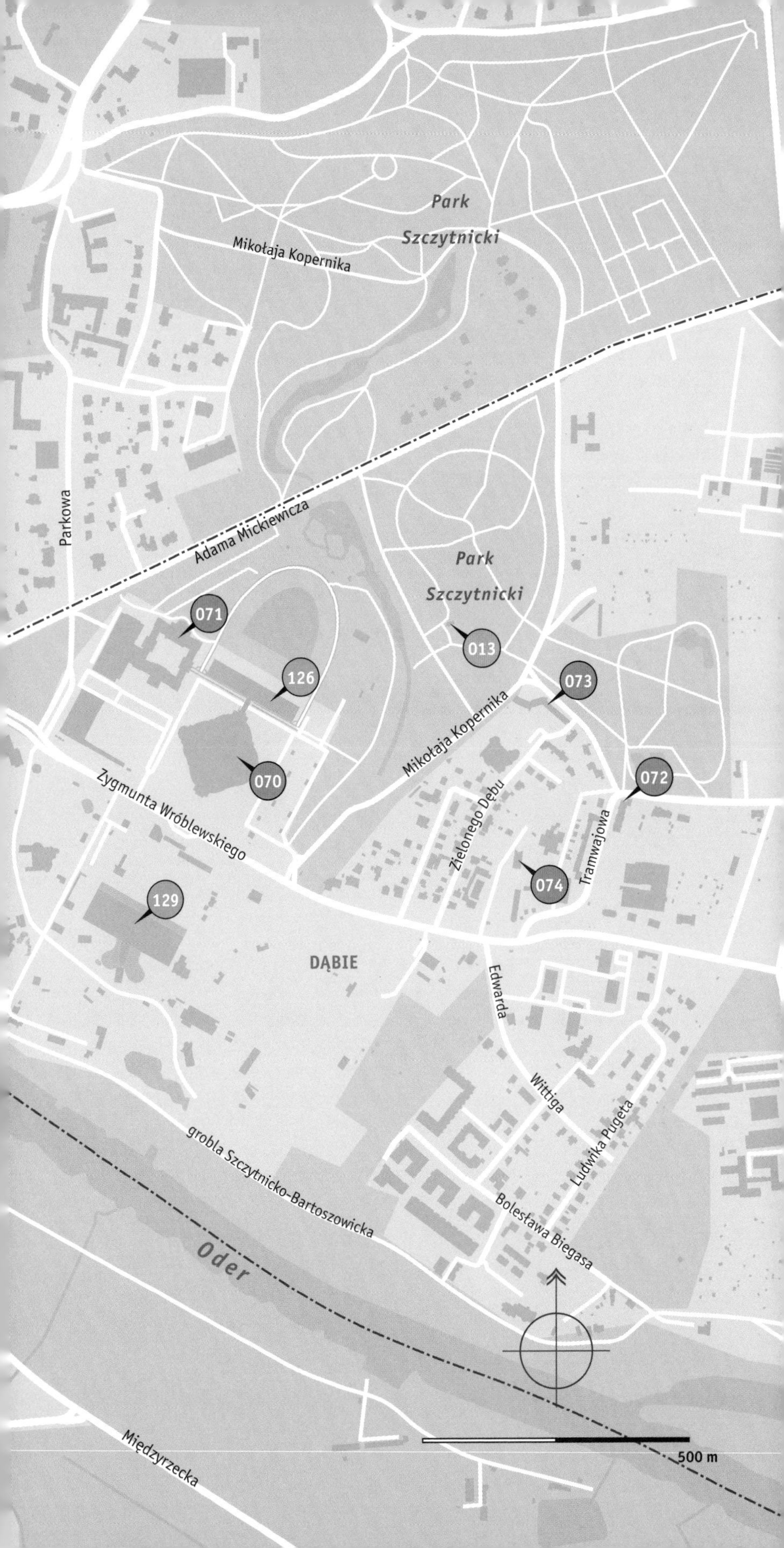
Park
Szczytnicki
Mikołaja Kopernika
Park
Szczytnicki
Adama Mickiewicza
Parkowa
071
126
013
073
070
072
Mikołaja Kopernika
Zielonego Dębu
Tramwajowa
Zygmunta Wróblewskiego
074
129
DĄBIE
Edwarda
Wittiga
Ludwika Pugeta
grobla Szczytnicko-Bartoszowicka
Bolesława Biegasa
Oder
Międzyrzecka
500 m

Architects

Sorted by project number

Buildings

Sorted by project number

Kuba Snopek

Izabela Cichońska

Karolina Popera

Łukasz Kos

Nicholas W. Moore

Kamil Krawczyk

Marcin Szczelina

Author and Co-Authors

Izabela Cichońska
Izabela Cichońska completed her master's degree in architecture at Wrocław University of Technology. Her thesis was awarded *Graduation Project of the Year* in 2010 by the Polish Association of Architects.

Łukasz Kos
Łukasz Kos is an architect and co-founder of FOUR O NINE Architecture and Interiors. Kos graduated with honours from the University of Toronto's faculty of architecture, landscape and design.

Kamil Krawczyk
Kamil Krawczyk studied economics at the University of Wrocław. He is currently a marketing specialist for the School Sisters of Notre Dame and has been working as a tour guide in Wroclaw since 2010.

Nicholas W. Moore
Nicholas Moore practises research, design, and building. Since 2005, he has balanced his theoretical pursuits with fieldwork in stonemasonry construction. Moore is currently based in Seattle, USA.

Karolina Popera
Karolina Popera completed her bachelor's degree in architecture at Wrocław University of Technology. Karolina was shortlisted in the international REA Competition 2015 for her vision of the future city.

Kuba Snopek
Kuba Snopek is an architect and researcher. He graduated in urban planning at the Wrocław University of Technology and preservation at the Strelka Institute. He is an expert in Soviet mass housing.

Marcin Szczelina
Marcin Szczelina is an architectural critic and curator. He currently works as a correspondent for *Domus* magazine. Szczelina is a co-founder of *Architecture Snob* and the founder of Furheart Gallery.

The *Deutsche Nationalbibliothek* lists this publication in the *Deutsche Nationalbibliografie*; detailed bibliographic data are available at *http://dnb.d-nb.de*

ISBN 978-3-86922-426-8

Editor
Clarice Knowles

Maps
Katrin Soschinski

Design
Masako Tomokiyo

Printing
Tiger Printing (Hong Kong) Co., Ltd.
www.tigerprinting.hk